Lorene Cary's

BLACK ICE

"The African-American author typically publishes as a first book his or her autobiography....This is as true for such contemporary figures as Claude Brown, Maya Angelou, and, more recently, Itabari Njeri as it was for such historical figures as Frederick Douglass.

"In her own debut, Lorene Cary takes her place in that remarkable procession. Clear and glittering as a New Hampshire lake in winter, *Black Ice* is an education in itself."　　　—Henry Louis Gates, Jr.

"Ripe with meaning...this work is honest and eloquent and ultimately optimistic."　　　　　　　　　　　　—Ellen Goodman,
Los Angeles Times Book Review

"*Black Ice* is a gift, a meaningful coming-of-age story told with remarkable candor and insight....[It] is engrossing from page one, and is, in many ways, a paean to the human spirit."　　—*Detroit News*

"*Black Ice* is written in a unique style that is beautiful, brisk and laden with keen insight....Cary has touched the white world and broken it into a prism of color."　　　　　　　—*Cleveland Plain Dealer*

"A true and beautiful writer...*Black Ice*, like Frank Conroy's *Stoptime* or Geoffrey Wolff's *The Duke of Deception*, is one of the classic modern memoirs of growing up in America."　　　—*Boston Globe*

BLACK ICE

Lorene Cary

BLACK ICE

Vintage Books
A Division of Random House, Inc.
New York

FIRST VINTAGE BOOKS EDITION, FEBRUARY 1992

Grateful acknowledgment is made to the following for permission to reprint
previously published material:

IRVING BERLIN MUSIC COMPANY: Excerpt from "Anything You Can Do" by
Irving Berlin. Copyright © 1946 by Irving Berlin. Copyright renewed.
Used by permission. International copyright secured. All rights reserved.

BUCK KILLETTE, SUNCOAST MUSIC (BMI): Excerpt from "Girl Watcher"
by Buck Killette. Copyright © 1968. Reprinted by permission.

MCA MUSIC PUBLISHING AND BOURNE CO. MUSIC PUBLISHERS: Excerpt from "Our
Day Will Come," words by Bob Hilliard and music by Mort Garson. Copyright
© 1963 (renewed), 1976 by MCA Music Publishing, a division of MCA Inc.,
New York, NY 10019, and Better Half Music Co. All rights reserved.
Used by permission of the copyright owners.

THE PUTNAM BERKLEY GROUP INC.: "I think I can, I think I can" from
The Little Engine That Could is a trademark of Platt & Munk and is reprinted
by permission of The Putnam Berkley Group Inc.

Library of Congress Cataloging-in-Publication Data
Cary, Lorene.
Black ice/Lorene Cary.—1st Vintage Books ed.
p.   cm.
ISBN 0-679-73745-6 (pbk).
1. Cary, Lorene.   2. Afro-American women—New Hampshire—Concord—
Biography.   3. Afro-Americans—New Hampshire—Concord—Biography.
4. Concord (N.H.)—Biography.   5. Afro-Americans—Education (Secondary)—
New Hampshire—Concord.   6. St. Paul's School (Concord, N.H.)   I. Title.
[F44.C7C44   1992]
373.18'296073-dc20   91-50489
CIP

Manufactured in the United States of America
579C86

To Laura Hagans Smith

Shall it any longer be said of the daughters
of Africa, they have no ambition . . . ?

Maria W. Stewart in *The Liberator*, 1831

. . . There is a grace in life. Otherwise we
could not live.

Paul Tillich, *The Shaking of the Foundations*

"Skin, skin, ya na know me?"

West Indian folktale

BLACK ICE

June 1989

I could see them from the dais: families and friends sitting on the risers, young students spilling out onto the grass, black-robed faculty members standing in front of their seats— all watching for the first graduates to begin their march down the grassy aisle between the folding chairs on the green. Someone let out a whoop as they appeared, the girls in their white dresses and the boys in their jackets and ties.

Fifteen years before I had walked down the same aisle as a graduate, and nine years later as a teacher. Now I was ending my term as a trustee.

I watched the black and Hispanic students, "my kids," come to the podium to receive their diplomas and awards from the Rector. One young man named Harlem winked at me as he passed. His shoulders still rocked a little, just a little, like the shoulders of black men in cities, and he held himself up on the balls of his feet like the ballet dancer he had become while at St. Paul's School. I remembered him as a Fourth Former, his head cocked to one side, asking, "I'd like to know: would you send *your* daughter to St. Paul's?"

The other students had laughed in that way that teenagers do when an adult is forced to reveal herself. But we also laughed together as black people alone, safe for the moment within the group, the collective tensions and harmonic humor of it, relieved for an hour or so from our headlong rush toward individual achievement.

"My daughter will have to decide that for herself," I said. "Don't you roll your eyes. I mean it. My parents did not make me come here. I was bound and determined. They *let* me, and it was not an easy thing to do.

"It won't be the same for my daughter. Neither my parents nor I really knew what we were getting into. Once you've made the journey, you can't pretend it didn't happen, that everything's like it was before except now you play lacrosse."

I had pretended, myself; many of us had. I had acknowledged my academic debt to the boarding school I'd attended on scholarship for two years. But I would not admit how profoundly St. Paul's had shaken me, or how damaged and fraudulent and traitorous I felt when I graduated. In fact, I pretended for so long that by the time I was twenty-six years old, I was able to convince myself that going back to school to teach would be the career equivalent of summering with distant, rich relatives.

Instead, I found my own adolescence, in all its hormonal excess, waiting for me at St. Paul's: old rage and fear, ambition, self-consciousness, love, curiosity, energy, hate, envy, compulsion, fatigue. I saw my adolescence in my students, and I felt it burbling inside me, grown powerful by long silence. I lost control of it one night when a black boy came to me nearly weeping because a group of white friends had told a racist joke in his presence. He hated himself, he said, because he hadn't known how to react. "It was like I couldn't move. I couldn't *do* anything," he said.

I too had known that terrible paralysis, and when the boy left, I wept with remembering. I could no longer forget, not with Westminster chimes ringing out the quarter hours, the piney mist that rolled off the pond in the morning, and the squeaking boards under our feet as we crossed Upper Common

Room to the dining hall. I remembered the self-loathing, made worse by a poised bravado, as close as my own skin, that I wore over it. I remembered duty and obligation—to my family, to the memory of dead relatives, to my people. And I remembered confusion: was it true that these teachers expected less of me than of my white peers? Or had I mistaken kindness for condescension? Were we black kids a social experiment? If we failed (or succeeded too well) would they call us off? Were we imported to help round out the white kids' education? Did it make any difference if we were?

In the aftermath of Black Is Beautiful, I began to feel black and blue, big and black, black and ugly. Had they done that to me? Had somebody else? Had I let them? Could I stop the feelings? Or hide them?

I knew that I was to emerge from St. Paul's School changed, but I did not know how, and I did not trust my white teachers and guardians to guide me. What would this education do to me? And what was I to do with it?

A couple years after I taught at St. Paul's, I was asked to serve as a trustee. During my term, I visited the school for board meetings, and I talked with the students. I could feel their attention one fall evening when I told them to try to think of St. Paul's as their school, too, not as a white place where they were trespassing. The next fall a boy told me: "I *had* been thinking of it as their school. It was like I had forgotten that this is my life."

Two years later that boy's formmates elected him class president. At his graduation, Eric smiled broadly at me as he walked to the podium to receive the President's Medal. So did a girl, an excellent and feisty writer, who was awarded the Rector's Medal. I wondered if they knew, or if they would learn, that just as St. Paul's was theirs, because they had attended the school and contributed to it, so, too, was American life and culture theirs, because they were black people in America.

Sitting on the dais, I recalled how wary I'd been of John
Walker, the first black teacher at St. Paul's, its first black
trustee, and the first black Bishop of the Washington, D.C.
diocese of the Episcopal Church. I remembered watching him
walk with other board members and trying to deduce from his
gait and the way he inclined his head whether the small man
with the tiny eyes was traitor or advocate.

He was still on the board during my tenure, a quiet-spoken
man who affected people deeply by his presence. John Walker
spoke wisely and from experience, but more than that, he em-
anated both judgment and compassion. I saw him affect my
colleagues. I felt him. He filled me with hope for my own racial
and spiritual healing, and courage to look back. (John Walker
died in September, 1989.)

I began writing about St. Paul's School when I stopped
thinking of my prep-school experience as an aberration from
the common run of black life in America. The isolation I'd felt
was an illusion, and it can take time and, as they say at St.
Paul's, "the love and labor of many," to get free of illusions.
The narratives that helped me, that kept me company, along
with the living, breathing people in my life, were those that
talked honestly about growing up black in America. They burst
into my silence, and in my head, they shouted and chattered
and whispered and sang together. I am writing this book to
become part of that unruly conversation, and to bring my experience back to the community of minds that made it possible.

"You must really love the school to be on the board." The
students wanted to know each time I visited. Each time I answered yes.

"Did you like it when you were here?"

I made a sour face. They looked relieved.

Chapter One

I had never heard of St. Paul's School until Mrs. Evans rang to tell me about it one fall night in 1971. I had just come home from Woolworth's, where I worked at the cheap-and-greasy fountain on Friday nights and Saturdays in a town my friends and I called "Tacky" Darby. I smelled as if I had scrubbed the grill with my uniform. My face shone with hamburger fat, and my Earth Shoes were spattered. At fourteen years old, I felt irritable and entitled to it, as adults seemed to be when they finished their work for the day.

Mrs. Evans's voice brimmed with excitement and fun. She was our next-door neighbor, a retired kindergarten teacher married to a newspaper reporter who had been the first black man on staff at the Philadelphia *Bulletin.* Three years before, when I was eleven, he had given me my first typewriter, a straight-back, black Underwood. Mrs. Evans was witty and down-to-earth, firm but easygoing with children. Her eyesight was poor; she had a recurring tickle that caused her to clear her throat nearly to gagging; under her shiny skin her knuckles were gnarled—yet she glowed with health. My father said that she had better legs than most thirty-year-olds, and my mother asked her advice. My sister, Carole, ran away to the brick house where a plaster Venus arose from her seashell and dolphins leapt at half-moons in the cream-colored ceiling molding. It was a fairy-tale house, and Mrs. Evans was a fairy godmother to us, distant and charming. I forgot that at first. Instead, I cradled the receiver on my shoulder and counted my tips while she talked, laying the coins silently on the kitchen counter.

Mrs. Evans had been told about St. Paul's School by a "lovely woman"—I took that to mean someone white, but trustworthy. This "very exclusive boarding school" had recently gone coed, and they were interested in finding black girls, too, so they'd put out the word with alumni and friends. Mrs. Evans had never visited the school, but she knew that the campus would be beautiful, that there would be music and languages and the arts. She also knew that scholarships—generous scholarships—were available. Mrs. Evans gave me the phone number of an alumnus, a judge, to call for more information. I wrote it down, thanked her for thinking of me, and went upstairs. I didn't need another school, I thought. I needed a bath.

Later that night, despite my adolescent defiance, I could not help but think about what Mrs. Evans had said. This education was more than knowledge; it could mean credentials, self-confidence, power. I imagined living away from home, making a precocious launch into the wide world of competition.

On Monday after school, I hurried home to call the judge, but when I got there, all I could do was stand next to the telephone preparing statements. My mother watched me as she cooked dinner. "Did Mrs. Evans give you the number to his home or his chambers?" she asked.

I hadn't thought about "chambers." Did "chambers" have telephones? I imagined a Dickensian suite of rooms, wood-paneled and dark, and in the middle a big, florid man draped in black robes, pondering important papers, a man who was not used to being interrupted by phone calls from strange fourteen-year-old black girls who wanted to go to his alma mater.

My mother laughed at me as I stood by the telephone in the kitchen staring at the number. "Just call him," she said.

Wherever I rang, the judge did not answer. A woman took the message and said that he would get back to me. We got on with dinner preparation. Our TV blared. Pots crackled, and dishes clattered; my parents talked over the TV; my eight-year-old sister talked over my parents; I talked over my sister. Then the telephone rang.

By the time I had motioned wildly for silence, the conversation was nearly finished. The judge said that he was pleased to hear of my interest. Then he gave me the name and address of another alumnus who would be hosting a meeting, and urged me to attend.

The meeting took place within a couple weeks. We drove through West Philadelphia, past the squat row houses where I had been raised, past the city center and then north where Wissahickon Creek falls away from the road, and woods rise up behind it. We were headed toward Chestnut Hill, more a place name than a place for me until then, a symbol of money and social exclusiveness. My father steered us through Germantown, where wet leaves lay in treacherous layers over trolley tracks and cobblestones. Cars slipped on and off the rails and then swerved to avoid each other, making rubbery squeals and muffled thuds.

By the time we pulled into the stone driveway, I felt as if we were a long way away from our home in the west end of Yeadon, an enclave of black professionals, paraprofessionals, wish-they-was-, look-like-, and might-as-well-be professionals, as we called ourselves. We were far away from the black suburb that, as a West Philly transplant, I disliked for its self-satisfied smugness. When we'd moved from our city apartment—from the living room with a convertible couch where my parents slept, from the bedroom where my sister and I slept (which was transformed into a dining room at Christmas), and from the kitchen where we normally ate, and where my mother pressed and curled women's hair in the evenings—Yeadon had impressed

me with its leafy green grandeur and insularity. But now, as
we stood in the Chestnut Hill driveway, I saw how modest our
Tudors were, our semidetached Dutch colonials, our muddy
driveways and the cyclone fences that held in our dogs. I saw
it then, with eyes made keen by years of witnessing our mer-
ciless self-criticism: "What's wrong with the colored race? I'll
tell you what's wrong with the colored race. We don't *think*.
That's what. And we do not stick together. And money? Forget
it. Invest? Get outta here. Now you take a look at the Jews. Or
you take the Chinese. . . ." I saw how consumed we'd been with
ambition, and how modest had been our goals.

Inside the stone house, in a large living room, we joined a
few other black people who had also come to learn about the
School. A boy who was younger than I sat next to his mother.
When I said hello, he did not turn his head to look at me, but
only peeped out of the corner of his eyes and nodded, as if we
might bolt out of the house together and go howling into the
Chestnut Hill woods if we were to look too hard at each other.
His mother, her hair done up like Coretta Scott King's, sat still
like her son. She looked as dignified as a picture on the back
of a church fan, and just as inanimate. If she kept any unauthorized verb forms from flying out from between her lips, she
also held in any sign of life.

Jeremy Price (this name and a few others have been changed),
a black teacher from St. Paul's, tried a few times to make small
talk, but he was a Brahmin from another planet: cool, ironic,
aloof. He was in his thirties, tweed-jacketed and bearded, with
a round belly. He touched his body lightly with his fingers, as
if he were not used to his own girth. In every other way he
appeared absolutely smooth and easy to my adolescent eye, and
assured to the point of arrogance.

Mr. Price made quick judgments of us; they showed in his
eyes. Clearly, the pillar-of-the-church lady with the Southern
coif (and Southern diffidence in the presence of white folks)

wasn't his type. Mr. Price seemed about to say something bru-
tal to her. My father stepped in to ask if he could join them.
The look she gave Daddy went beyond grateful to adoring.

Women looked at my father that way. Their attention seemed
to affect him as naturally as sunshine—and he never talked too
much. "Still water runs deep," my great-grandmother had said
about him when he came courting; she said so until she died.
Men saw more ripples on the pond, which those of us who
lived with him knew positively were caused by undertows.

For one thing, when men exchanged the inevitable sports
conversation they discovered, as Mr. Price did, that my father
was a student of judo. He'd spent three nights a week since his
twenty-eighth birthday at the dojo. He had progressed from
white belt to brown to black. We'd gone to competitions
throughout the mid-Atlantic region, and I'd watched three-
minute dramas on the mat. Each time he had to beat or be
beaten. In contest after contest he was a light-middleweight
whose feet made the sound of rushing as they swept the dry
mat and whose face turned purple when the last man, the one
he finally could not beat, held him down, cutting into his wind-
pipe with his bleached white *gi*. In those moments, when I
prayed that he would not be killed in some fluke throw, I saw
in his eyes a concentration and force that made life with us in
the sparkling three-room apartment seem like some errant
choice. He was, above all, a physical being, a wiry man who
once tied our deluxe-size refrigerator to his back to move it,
and would probably not object to being remembered that way.
We three, two girls and a woman, surrounded him with doll
babies and crisscross curtains. It was like watching a carnivore
sit down to porridge each night.

Dad had first seen judo practiced in a 1945 film, *Blood on the
Sun,* with James Cagney. Intended as anti-Japanese propa-
ganda, the film showed an expansionist culture, arrogant and
absolute. Daddy loved it. Judo: there was a vision of power—

mental, physical, spiritual—beneath a placid exterior. It was nearly twenty years before my father stepped onto a mat. Now, he only needed to mention the word. People looked at him as if he had jumped out of a Samurai movie. Even Mr. Price lost his frost when the subject came up. As I watched the two of them chat, my fear of Mr. Price dissipated, but not my wariness. He did not quite seem one of us.

Mike Russell did. He was a St. Paul's School senior recruiting black candidates as an independent-study project, and he had more poise than I'd ever seen in a teenager. His skin was chocolatey and fine-pored, and his bottom lip pouted like Sidney Poitier's. He was sleek and articulate. He paid attention to me.

I crossed my legs with what I hoped was lithe grace and stretched my neck until I nearly pitched forward onto the floor. I wanted to know the things he must know: about science and literature and language, living away from home, New England, white people, money, power, himself. I supposed that the other black students at St. Paul's must have had Russell's sophistication and charm, his commitment to black progress.

I had to be part of that. With the force of religious conversion, the great God of education moved within me, an African Methodist God with a voice that boomed like thunder. It took all my strength to hold myself inside my skin. This school— why, this was what I had been raised for, only I hadn't known it. They closed the curtains and turned off the lights for the slide show. I hoped that my face had not betrayed me.

Russell narrated the slide show. He told us about the Old Chapel, a steepled red-brick church, and towering behind it on the green lawn, the Chapel of St. Peter and St. Paul, built in 1886 to accommodate a larger student body, and enlarged in 1927. The New Chapel was massive. Its brick and stone walls were heavy and stolid; and yet its stained-glass windows seemed infinitely light, as if they could almost float up to the heavens.

We saw other buildings as well: the Schoolhouse, student houses (in keeping with the school's family-centered lexicon, they were not to be called dormitories), the Rectory, the funny circular post office, and special academic buildings for science, math, and art. The gray granite library with its white columns had been built by somebody famous. It sat at the edge of yet another pond, casting a wavering, silvery reflection on the water.

Over and over again we saw these buildings, draped with scenic young people, alone or in small groups, talking, laughing, bending their heads toward one another or running together on a green field in some pantomime of benevolent competition. I saw black boys. I saw girls, a few of them black, too. And I saw them all in a brilliant medley of New Hampshire seasons. At one point in the slide show, Russell flashed through the carousel to find a misplaced slide, creating an intoxicating display of colors—autumn red and gold, winter snowy blue-white, spring green and pink and blue—so sharp and bright that they seemed to originate not on the screen, but from deep inside my head, like music.

Mr. Price's voice, clear and insouciant, brought me back to myself. He was asking for someone to open the drapes.

My mother began with a question about the progress of co-education. First there were tea dances, Mr. Price said, begun in the nineteenth century and carried forward into the 1960s as dance weekends. Girls were bused in, talked to, danced with, and then bused out again. He looked at Mike Russell and asked ironically, "How were they?"

Russell shook his head and laughed. "They were awful!"

Mr. Price went on. In 1969 and 1970, girls came, like foreigners, to participate in a winter-term exchange. The next winter, the first nineteen came to stay.

What was a tea dance? I wondered. Tea meant little girls with clean hands and faces sipping out of china cups, eating butter cookies with raspberry jam. Teas belonged in church or in childhood. A dance, to the contrary, meant teenagers in a basement: black lights, red bulbs, music jamming its way through our shoes and up into our feet. It meant arms in the air, whistles, a soul train down the middle of the room, whipping out new steps nice and casual as if we hadn't spent all week practicing. It meant sweat steaming out of the tops of our heads, shrinking Afros worthy of Angela Davis down to dreaded TWAs (teeny weeny Afros). A dance meant watching sharp so that no amorous brother spoiled our hot pants.

Tea had nothing to do with it.

Mr. Price acted as cultural interpreter for us, as if a bank of white and black computers stood on either side of him, bleeping away in incompatible languages. When my mother asked about the grading system, I heard her asking whether white teachers four hundred miles away would give her kid a fair grade. Hanging in the air was our fear that they'd let us survive, but never excel. Mr. Price answered by describing the system: High Honors for work that was truly outstanding; Honors for work that was very, very good; High Pass—he laughed and shook his head—was a great, gray, muddy area between the very good and the OK; Pass was just acceptable; and Unsatisfactory was "self-explanatory." Then he estimated how many students received which grades, and quite directly—said it right out in this white alumnus's house with the costly furnishings—told us how the black students were doing. He said most of them were working hard, but some were not, frankly, getting what the school had to offer. He did not answer the black mothers' fear of their children's powerlessness, their vulnerability to white adults who might equate sharpness of the mind with sharpness of features.

Mr. Price encouraged Russell to comment. Mike told a few stories about himself, portraying St. Paul's as a place where well-meaning, well-trained teachers tried hard to live up to their calling. Some, he added meaningfully, were more sensitive than others.

Then my mother told a story about a science award I had won in third grade. She started with the winning—the long, white staircase in the auditorium of the Franklin Institute, and how the announcer called my name twice because we were way at the back and it took me so long to get down those steps.

Mama's eyes glowed. She was a born raconteur, able to increase the intensity of her own presence and fill the room. She was also a woman who seldom found new audiences for her anecdotes, so she made herself happy, she insisted, with us children, her mother, her sisters, her grandparents—an entire clan of storytellers competing for a turn on the family stage. This time all eyes were on my mother. Her body, brown and plump and smooth, was shot through with energy. This time the story had a purpose.

She told them how my science experiment almost did not get considered in the citywide competition. My third-grade teacher, angry that I'd forgotten to bring a large box for displaying and storing the experiment, made me pack it up to take home. (Our teacher had told us that the boxes were needed to carry the experiments from our class to the exhibition room, and she'd emphasized that she would not be responsible for finding thirty boxes on the day of the fair. Without a box, the experiment would have to go home. Other kids, white kids, had forgotten boxes during the week. They'd brought boxes the next day. I asked for the same dispensation, but was denied. The next day was the fair, she said. That was different.)

I came out of school carrying the pieces of the experiment my father had picked out for me from a textbook. This was a simple buoyancy experiment where I weighed each object in the air and then in water, to prove that they weighed less in water. I had with me the scale, a brick, a piece of wood, a bucket, and a carefully lettered poster.

Well, my mother marched me and my armload of buoyant materials right back into school and caught the teacher before she left. The box was the only problem? Just the box? Nothing wrong with the experiment? An excited eight-year-old had forgotten a lousy, stinking box that you get from the supermarket, and for that, she was out of the running? The teacher said I had to learn to follow directions. My mother argued that I had followed directions by doing the experiment by myself, which was more than you could say for third graders who'd brought in dry-cell batteries that lit light bulbs and papier-mâché volcanoes that belched colored lava.

"Don't you ever put me in a position like that again," Mama said when we were out of earshot of the classroom. "You never know who is just waiting for an excuse to shut us out."

We got the box; my experiment went into the fair; I won the prize at school. I won third prize for my age group in the city.

My ears began to burn. I could not help but believe that they would see through this transparent plug, and before I had even laid hands on an application. They'd think we were forward and pushy. I forgot, for the moment, how relieved I'd felt when Mama had stood in front of that teacher defending me with a blinding righteousness, letting the teacher know that I was not as small and black and alone as I seemed, that I came from somewhere, and where I came from, she'd better believe, somebody was home.

The other mothers nodded approvingly. My father gave me a wide, clever-girl smile. Mr. Price and Russell looked at me deadpan. They seemed amused by my embarrassment.

The story was an answer, part rebuke and part condolence, to Mike Russell's stories, where no parents figured at all. It was a message to Mr. Price about her maternal concerns, and a way to prove that racism was not some vanquished enemy, but a real, live person, up in your face, ready, for no apparent reason, to mess with your kid. When I was in third grade, and her marriage to my father had looked like forever, when Martin Luther King was alive preaching love, and white flight had not yet sunk the real-estate values in West Philly, Mama could do her maternal duty, and face down a white teacher who would have deprived me of my award. Who at St. Paul's School would stand up for her child in her stead?

Mr. Price did not answer my mother's story. Instead he invited a few more questions. The Mama's boy asked about food and mosquitoes and telephones. He looked appalled to hear that there were no phones in the rooms, only public phone booths outside, and only a handful at that. I doubted that I'd see that child again.

If we wanted to be considered for candidacy, we were to write for an application, our own letters, composed in our own hand, and register to take standardized tests. In addition, Mr. Price said, it would be worth our while to visit the school in person.

Our host, Ralph Starr, who had slipped out of the room during the discussion, had slipped back in. Mr. Price thanked him for the use of his house. Mr. Starr took exception. He was glad to be able to help in the good work that Mr. Price and Mike were doing. In fact he thanked *us* for coming. The adults appeared pleased. They chatted with each other; I talked to Mike, and the session ended.

As we drove away, my mother could not get over how Mrs. Starr had given her barefoot toddler a spoonful of peanut butter to lick before she was spirited upstairs. Mama didn't feed us peanut butter. It wasn't proper good food, she said. It was what PWTs—poor white trash—gave their kids. For my lunch, Mom packed baked chicken on toast with lettuce and mayonnaise, ham, tuna, sliced tongue, or cheese.

I was as jolted by the sight as my mother, and not just the peanut butter, but the whole family scene. I had thought that rich white people would have been quieter, their children more tidy, their mothers less vibrant. I didn't like it that my mother, too, had been surprised. It made me nervous.

A week later, however, I did not think of the background kid-babble in Chestnut Hill, but of the wide drawing room and the slides. Mr. Price wrote promptly to inform us that he had indeed scheduled the visit we'd said we wanted to make to the school.

"They don't play, do they?" My parents took turns asking each other and answering back.

"Those people do not play."

Chapter Two

From inside my grandparents' vestibule, with two fingers hooked loosely over her bottom teeth, Carole watched us drive off for New Hampshire. I saw my grandmother whisper in her ear, and I knew that her voice would be full of indulgent promise.

We headed toward the New Jersey Turnpike, the beginning, for Philadelphians, of every trip north. The turnpike's smooth black asphalt whirred under our tires. I settled into my seat. Although there was no longer the old intimacy among the three of us, there was the same symmetry—Dad driving; Mama next to him, her hand flung over his headrest and flicking occasionally like the tail of a cat; me, alone, in the back. Suburbs gave way to small farms covered with the frozen stubble of cornstalks and bare fruit trees. It was December. We laughed about how much colder New Hampshire would be. Excitement spread inside me, hot and frightening, like dye injected into a vein.

"You're going to be mighty glad you packed those knee socks," my mother said with feigned neutrality.

The sock contest had started simply enough. I had been packing when my mother came into my room and saw my stockings folded on the bed next to the suitcase. Those would have to stay home, she said, picking them up and moving them back to the bureau. Knee socks were the thing to wear to this kind of place, she said; knee socks were "classic." Then she laid a look on me: indulgent, ready to get mad, amused, annoyed, threatening.

Every mother I knew had that look. It had been the first one I can remember mocking. Later my friends and I all did it together. "Don't start with me," we'd tell each other.

"Don't *you* start."

"Don't even *try* it."

Womanish among ourselves, we were silent before the women themselves. We used a tame version of our bored eyes (which were their eyes as we saw them, bored with us and the childishness of our antics) against them, but we obeyed.

I packed the knee socks, and I packed the stockings, too. They were mine. I'd bought them with my money, the money I made at the five-and-ten where I watched the fountain supervisor trim bitten ends off half-eaten hot dogs, rinse and then plop them into the Coney Island soup. I'd earned those stockings, and I wanted them with me.

Near Elizabeth a clingy stink seeped in through the heating vents. Sulphurous and sweet, filthy and dense, the pollution poured from the landscape: refineries burned oil and coal; a slaughterhouse dumped bloody spoilage doused with formaldehyde; landfills oozed bilge into a river named Kill. When the heating system seemed about to choke us, we had no choice but to open the windows, and let the air, laden with its cold, moist stink, wash over us.

"Money," my mother said, motioning toward the wasteland around us. "What America will do for a buck."

We drove through New York City, past the projects of the south Bronx, where people hung their laundry to be dried by the exhaust fumes, and past the north Bronx, with its boxy co-ops and the clean-block neighborhoods where my cousins lived.

The sun dropped off the edge of the earth just behind us and to the left. Within moments, it had snatched the last friendly glow from the sky. Around us, headlights of passing cars carved cylindrical plugs out of the darkness, each separate, apart, lighting only enough road to see its own way through.

"This is a *wide* state." So my parents told each other as we drove through Connecticut. Massachusetts came and went. After nearly eight hours on the road, we crossed the state line into New Hampshire. Well-maintained highways cut through granite cliffs and black woods. Small mountains of bulldozed snow lined the shoulders. Nashua and then Manchester erupted out of the land, little citylets whose worn factories hulked along the Merrimack River. We could not tell which were abandoned, and which, when daylight broke, would be alive with workers.

Concord, New Hampshire, had no such industrial district. Its Main Street swept us into a three- and four-story-tall town center. Pleasant Street took us out again, west, toward the school. To our left we saw a simple white sign with black letters. It said: St. Paul's School.

Once onto the grounds, our car bucked and lurched across the rutty ice to Scudder House, a white clapboard cottage with brick chimneys and dark green shutters. The front door was unlocked. We opened it and stepped in. A spectacled gentleman with a handlebar mustache regarded us from the far wall.

"Who is he?" asked my mother.

I read the brass nameplate: "Willard Scudder."

"Well, who else would he be?"

We walked into a light green bedroom with twin beds, where my father deposited their bags, and past the tiny kitchen to a peach-colored bedroom, same beds, where I put mine. A note in the kitchen invited us to help ourselves to soft drinks. More notes in the bedrooms explained how to turn on the electric blankets. I was afraid to sleep underneath live electric wires, but the guesthouse, charming and well appointed, was cold. I turned the dial. Warmth spread over me. I drifted off into a luxurious, and yet disconcerted, sleep.

The smell of frying bacon and the sound of a stranger's voice woke me.

"What kind of juice would you like?" The housekeeper spoke in a thin voice; it emerged from a rib cage no bigger around than a twelve-year-old's. Three years later, in the same kitchen, this woman would hand me a graduation card permeated by the inky smell of a fresh five-dollar bill. Eight years after that, when I returned to teach, she would stand in the same narrow kitchen, tiny shoulders silhouetted against the same window, and stare into my face to find the plumper, younger face concealed. She would share with me her loneliness after her husband's death: the stillness of the air inside her house, the pointlessness of unused chairs, days off with nothing to do. Narrowing her eyes to look back, she'd remember my mother, too.

I heard them talk that December morning while I dressed. "Please, don't bother with that," my mother said.

"No bother."

"Now, with a living room this size, they must use Scudder for more than a guesthouse. This room would be perfect for a banquet—a small banquet—or a luncheon."

"Yep. We do serve some big meals here."

"You don't mean to tell me they make you do any real *cooking* in a kitchen this size?"

"Nope. I don't cook it."

"I was going to say. . . ."

"Cafeteria sends the food up. The van comes right to that back door there. I serve it, buffet-style. They serve themselves. I clean up."

She stayed in the kitchen while we ate, self-consciously, at the drop-leaf table under Mr. Scudder's portrait. I assumed he was appalled, and I was pleased to think so.

Mike Russell appeared to take us for a tour of the grounds and buildings. They were little more to me than a backdrop to our own improbable drama. Russell could have been leading me through the Land of the Sweets, I was so dreamy. He'd be gone by the time I got in, *if* I got in, I kept reminding myself, trying not to lose control. Like a tourist in a foreign country, I felt that it might be possible to come to this school and be free of my past, free to re-create myself. I smiled at Russell as he guided us into the New Chapel. He did not know that on a bet I'd eaten half a worm in fifth grade, and up here there'd be nobody to tell him or anyone else.

From the antechapel we looked down a long aisle flanked on either side by three rows of graduated pews for students and high-backed seats carved into the walls for teachers. The floors were laid with brick-colored quarry tile. At the end of the center aisle, the altar rose distant and ornate. Slants of sunbeams were colored by tall stained-glass windows overhead. To our left a bright white marble angel cradled an equally white nude in muscular tribute to the school's war dead.

My head filled with the words and melodies of familiar prayers: the doxology, the Lord's Prayer, snippets of music:

> *My soul be on thy guard*
> *Ten thousand foes arise:*
> *And hosts of sin are pressing hard*
> *To drive thee from the skies.*

In the African Methodist Episcopal church, the minister would continue: "Honor thy father and thy mother that thy days may be long upon the land that the Lord thy God giveth thee." I heard the music, punctuated by the creaking pews, in my head. I heard the floor of Ward A.M.E. groan under its red carpet as the parishioners lined up in the aisle to take their burdens to the Lord. We touched hands and hugged each other as we made our slow progress toward the altar.

In the Chapel of St. Peter and St. Paul the heels of our shoes clicked on the stone floors. The aisle was wide enough for a mummers' procession. My music would not fit here. Neither would my God, He whom I had held onto, just barely, through the music that spoke comfort and retribution, and the community, the perfumed and bosomy women who approved of me, and the old men who nodded at me each Sunday. I could not conjure my God in this place, and it seemed His failure. Surprise, as cold as the electric blanket had been warm, overwhelmed me. We left the chapel. It was time for my interview.

Inside the Schoolhouse, at the top of a slate staircase, was a waiting room where Russell handed us over to Mr. Price. I smelled coffee brewing, and I heard classroom sounds— discussion, laughter, lecturing, but no shouts or threats, no yardsticks banging for silence, no words of shame or derision. My father, who taught in a public junior high school, looked away from Mr. Price and my mother for a moment and smilingly shook his head.

Our admissions officer, Mr. Dick, came into the waiting room. After a general greeting, he ushered us into an office and closed the door. This was what we had come for, and it was nothing like I had imagined.

For one thing, I had not expected my parents to be invited into my interview. Once they were in, I could not keep my eyes off them. They filled the room with their presence. Mr. Dick, I could see, was impressed by them. They were altogether natural, and yet larger than I'd ever seen them. My mother engaging and shiny-eyed, my father, thoughtful and imposing. They wanted St. Paul's, too—I saw that for the first time—or else they could not have created this portrayal of themselves: the ambitious couple in their thirties, grateful for an opportunity for their daughter, eager to help, reluctant to let her go. Why, St. Paul's, they said, was a dream come true, and I agreed. I loved to look at them like this. It was almost too good.

And yet it was true. I knew it. It was as true as the estrangement that had settled between them like chill damp in our basement. It was as true as our weekdays, morning after chaotic morning, when I looked in vain for the correct time on the faces of our several too-fast clocks, as my mother shouted up the stairs at approximately seven-forty-five that it was eight o'clock and we were late. Late! Always late. Always rushing, hobbled, baffled by the confusion that came our way. Whose fault? Whose?

And it was as true as our barely acknowledged disappointment in the big Yeadon house, which had not made us happier together, as I'd expected it would. Why else had we bought it? Why else the scrimping and saving, the thrift-shop furniture, the careful hand-washing of delicates, the parade of used, rather than new, auto parts?

I made a freeze-frame of my parents in my mind: big, expansive, generous, unhurried. It was what I had done as a child when I had felt in danger of getting too happy. I'd make a picture in my mind to go back to later and enjoy in bits. My mother was wearing her best lipstick, and my father sat content, wanting to be nowhere else but right there, with us. I made a picture of them like that—I can still see it—and I held my new gorgeous reverence for them way deep inside where it made me warm and giddy like brandy.

Then, Mr. Dick asked my parents to leave. Their interview was over. They had passed; how could they not? It was my turn, but I felt guilty that they should go. How could I sit alone in the office, discussing my worthiness for an education they'd never had? It was quiet after he'd shown them out. Quiet. It was hard to pull myself back, to stop watching others and start promoting myself. I wanted to watch some more. I wanted to look at Mr. Dick, his mannerisms, his eyes. I wanted to read his files and eavesdrop on his phone calls so I'd know who I was dealing with.

"Tell me, Lorene, what most attracts you to St. Paul's School?"

"I guess what I would look forward to most is being somewhere where all the students *want* to learn. In my school, if you get a really good report card, you feel like you better hide it on the way home."

It was partially true. Afraid of becoming an egghead and of appearing to be one, I smoked in the bathrooms, cursed regularly, and participated in mild pranks. But Yeadon High had plenty of ambitious kids of ambitious parents, and was hardly so tough a place as I insinuated. Mr. Dick did not seem to know that. I wondered what he thought it was like.

"It's not considered cool to do well?"

"Not really."

"And do you like school?"

"Most of the time, yes." A bald-faced lie. I disliked school, always had—the clanking institutional sounds in cavernous old buildings, the cheap dropped ceilings and multipurpose cafeteria-gymnasium-auditorium rooms in new ones. I hated fights. I was offended by standing in lines ("We're not moving until everybody is standing ab-so-lute-ly still"); insulted by teachers' condescension ("If you can't pronounce Mrs. *Rak-our,* you just call me Mrs. *Rock-over*"); I was numbed by busywork ("Copy pages five hundred and fifty-five through five hundred and fifty-eight from your dictionaries, and see if *that* can keep your traps shut"). I dreaded gym. Mr. Dick could tell that I was lying; he smiled.

When we got around to books, I was finally set, as our
minister would say, on solid ground. I gorged on books. I
sneaked them at night. I rubbed their spines and sniffed in the
musty smell of them in the library. I sped through my grandfather's paperbacks that lined the wall of their mint-green sun
parlor and read and reread the dirty parts until I was damp. I
memorized black poetry—stately sonnets, skittering bebop
rhymes, any celebration of black women—and I drank in the
fury of my contemporaries. I did not tell Mr. Dick that I'd
been reading *The Spook Who Sat by the Door,* or that I was attracted to the murderous rage of the protagonist, a token black
like me.

When my interview ended, Mr. Dick opened the door for
me. He held it while I stepped through. "I hope you're ready
for homework," he said. "Because there's plenty of it here."

Was he assuming that a black girl from public school might
not be up to it? I wondered. Or was I too sensitive? I'd been
told that before, and I knew it was true, but I couldn't always
tell when. Sometimes "sensitive" was what kids called each
other when they wanted license for cruelty, or what white people said when they did not want to bother to change.

"Really," he said as we walked toward the waiting room. "If
you would not look forward to three hours—and sometimes
more—of homework a day, then St. Paul's is the wrong
school."

"I do my homework," I said. It was too quick and too sharp.
I smiled to soften the defiance I'd let slip.

Mr. Dick reunited me with my parents. Once again we stood
in a group chatting. We had been chatting all weekend. Chat.
Chat. Chat. I could not think of one more thing to say. Not
one. I smiled. My temples were sore.

A buzzer sounded the change of period. Doors banged open,
and students swarmed the halls. A few girls walked by, but for
the most part the Schoolhouse teemed with boys. They were

tall and short, wiry, stocky, fat, skinny, loud, groomed, un-
kempt, babyish, manly—and they were white.

Then a group of black boys passed by. They stopped on the
second-floor landing. A couple of boys smiled. A couple looked
elsewhere. A couple looked me over. One boy, who was wearing a black leather jacket and cap, stepped forward.

"Well, hello there," he said. "Are you here to apply to St.
Paul's?"

I nodded. "Yes."

"Oh, wow! That's great. Where're you from?"

"Philadelphia."

"How about that? What's your name?"

"Aw, come on, Wood." The boys had been amused to watch
their buddy in action for a while. Now they wanted to move
on.

"You'll be gone next year, anyway."

"You'll have to excuse him," one of the boys said to me.

They laughed together and bounced in a group down the
steps. I was annoyed. I smiled again at the adults. My temples
were rigid with exertion.

Mr. Price appeared to take us to lunch. On the way we
stopped at his dorm. His modern apartment had tall windows
and bright white walls. He told my parents that the school paid
for faculty members to do graduate work in the summers and,
after a few years' teaching, to go to Europe. He showed us a
red-and-white china bowl depicting scenes from the grounds
that he was given after five years' service. My mother said that
my father should think about teaching at St. Paul's. I was appalled to hear it.

"It doesn't look like your daughter thinks that's a good idea,"
Mr. Price said. He enjoyed the joke and kept it going.

"We could use you," he said to my father, looking to me for
a reaction. "I'm sure we could arrange to have you put in his
class. Would you like that?"

I was relieved when, on the way to lunch, Mr. Price found another student to tease. "Alma Jean! Alma Jean!" Mr. Price mimicked a Southern accent and laughed at a girl at the top of the path. "Alma, come meet a visiting family."

The path sloped steeply. Underneath the sawdust, a thick crust of ice gave off the dull gray sheen of moonstone. Students going to and from lunch stepped around us. They slipped off the shoulder of the icy path and made giant steps into the surrounding snow. Two or three of them fell. They laughed at each other and slid away. I felt my toes curl under in my boots, even though I knew that nothing short of grappling hooks could save me if I began to fall. And, of course, my mother was holding onto my arm, smiling a blaze of new lipstick. Her fingers dug into my sleeve. God forbid one of us should slip. We'd both go down, brown behinds right up in the air for Mr. Price and all these white people to see, my father grabbing for both of us with some wild, involuntary cry from ancient Japan, my mother screaming, and everybody rushing to help us, their solicitude, the shrieks of hysterical laughter once they were out of earshot.

Alma Jean reached us alive. The door she'd come out of at the top of the path might as well have been cradled in the clouds. I'd never make it.

"Welcome to St. Paul's," Alma said. She was a short Southern girl with acne on her round cheeks, glasses, and a big, fluffy Afro the color of old honey. "I hope you had a good trip." She'd already taken in the knee socks, I could see that, and was now processing my "classic" getup in all its devoutly-wished-for understatement.

"This is Alma's first year," said Mr. Price. "She came here from Memphis, Tennessee, and she's in the Fourth Form." He looked down at her.

"Oh, you must miss home," my mother said.

"Yes, ma'am, I do."

"And it's a lot colder than you must be used to," Mama said. "Is that all you wear?"

Like the other students, Alma sported a jacket. We, of course, were swaddled in everything but buffalo hide.

"Yes, ma'am. They told me it was going to be cold up here, but nobody told me it would be *this* cold!"

I could see that Alma was a little feisty for my mother's taste in teenagers, but Mama couldn't help but go for that "ma'am" stuff. Mr. Price tried to steer Alma back to a proper discussion. "Now, Alma, aside from climate considerations, are you enjoying your first year here? Your classes, sports, activities?"

Alma giggled and rolled her eyes. Nope, she did not dig this place. She'd signified it, OK, and now I waited to hear the words that would disavow her look.

"Well, naw, not really, Mr. Price." She burst into quick laughter, but she stuck to her story. "I mean, this is an *excellent* education. The best. But 'like it'? I don't know if those would be my exact words."

I watched her leave, jealous of the cool disdain with which she looked up at Mr. Price and the way she bounded over the ice when she left, careless and confident as a cat.

We waved gingerly in Alma's direction. Then we turned, arms still locked, to begin our ascent. By the time we made it safely into the building, I had begun to sweat into my layers of wool.

We walked through a cold, bright cloister. On black iron hooks along the windows, jackets were hung to chill while their owners ate. We folded our coats—these were our good coats we were wearing—and laid them on benches by a wall that was covered with oak panels carved, like the panels in the Schoolhouse, with the names of graduates. Heaps of textbooks and paperbacks lay scattered on benches and the floor. Like toppling cairns they led us to the dining room.

The lunch line snaked through the Upper Common Room, past the formal dining hall with its dark, high-backed chairs and forbidding portraits, and into the kitchen. We collected trays and battered silver-plate utensils. In our turn we stepped up to be served. Behind a long steam table stood the poorest-looking white people I'd ever seen. These were residents of a state training school for the mentally retarded, Mr. Price explained. During the school terms they worked with the food-service staff and boarded in rooms above the kitchen. Students, for some reason, referred to them as wombats.

"But aside from that rather predictable teenage cruelty," said Mr. Price, "the kids, on the whole, treat the staff with at least a modicum of respect."

"Nice hot soup," said one of the women. Her teeth were rotten, and she showed them when she smiled.

It seemed wrong for these people to stand there, separated from us by chrome and glass and crusted-over sheet pans. It seemed wrong for them to remain stunted in the presence of growing, budding, blooming talent, able only to feed the young aristocrats who would go away and forget them. I took the bowl from the woman with the medieval mouth. There seemed nothing else I could do. Soup, thick with cornstarch, sloshed onto my thumb, and the woman apologized fast, like a child who has been beaten.

"Lost your appetite, eh?" Lee Bouton sat across from me at the lunch table. She was a year or two older than I, long and lean and unhurried. Her beige face was framed with nearly black hair, thick and wiry, pulled back into a big, Africanized bun. I would never have guessed—almost no one did—that Lee's mother was white, as were her older brother and her stepfather, a college professor. Years later Bouton called her urban black image a literary creation, one she'd absorbed from her peers and fashioned from books her stepfather had recommended.

A few other students sat with us. They were friendly, welcoming, quirky. I wondered if I'd displayed enough character in my interview. Perhaps the Yeadon High booklist I bragged that I'd read was as tacky as those fishnet stockings I had wanted to wear and insisted on packing. There was no solid ground up here for me, but neither was there any going back.

My parents and I repeated, as if it were just the right thing to say, that St. Paul's was a dream come true. During our stay the dream began to take on an aura of inevitability. I cradled my desire gingerly, as if I could keep it secret even from myself, but the visit had given me a feeling of necessity. I had to go to St. Paul's. I had been raised for it.

Why else had my mother personally petitioned the principal of Lea School so that I could attend the integrated showcase public grade school at the edge of the University of Pennsylvania's reach—out of our West Philly district? Why else would she have dragged me across the street on my knees when I balked on the morning before the big I.Q. test, the one that could get me into the top first-grade class, the class on which free instrument and French lessons, advanced Saturday-morning classes, and a special, individualized reading series were bestowed? I remembered the bandages, white and meticulous, covering the suppurating red flesh underneath. Why else had I learned to hold myself to standards that were always just beyond my reach, if not to learn early and indelibly that we'd have to do twice the work to get half the credit? Why the thrift-shop Dickens volumes, stiff and stinking with mildew, the Berlitz records, *Weekly Readers,* and Spanish flashcards? Why the phone call that night from Mrs. Evans? Hadn't I been told, hadn't they said all along, that each of us had work to do? Wasn't it time for me to play my part in that mammoth enterprise—the integration, the moral transformation, no less, of America?

I had been waiting for this the way a fairy princess waits for a man. But I'd never suspected that my fate would be revealed so handsomely or so soon.

By the time we arrived in New Jersey to pick up my sister, the events of my life had rearranged themselves in perfect anticipation of my beckoning academic career. I entered my grandparents' familiar home yearning to soak it in, as if part of me had already left.

We crowded into the cool aroma of the vestibule, where Nana kept her fruit in the winter, and then into the house. The cold air we brought in disturbed the quiet pale green rooms; pointed crystals that hung from pink-and-white lusters on the dining-room bureau swayed in the draft. They were antique glass lusters, older than I was, Nana had told me, made from opaque white glass over cranberry glass over crystal, the last of the fine cameo glass to come out of Czechoslovakia before the Communists took over. The lusters did not require candles in their cylindrical crystal centers. They needed only the light from elsewhere in the room, which reflected off their many surfaces. They were elegantly efficient, purely feminine, the most unnecessary objects in my universe. They caught my eye when we walked in. This time I was delighted to wonder how such a rich cranberry color could emanate from such fragile glass. They were as beautiful as anything I'd seen at St. Paul's, a gratifying thought.

In fact, something about St. Paul's reminded me of my grandparents. They belonged to clubs whose members were the old, genteel black Philadelphia, alternately called "dicty" or "blue-vein" years ago. My grandmother had inherited from her father a real-estate business whose profits provided scholarships for black college students. My grandfather had played semipro baseball in the Negro leagues. He worked in a corporate sales job where he earned, he said, not as much as he would have had he been white, but more than he would had he looked black. He was the only person I knew who loved to go to work. That's how I wanted to feel about school.

Carole ran down the stairs and hugged me. We had missed each other, and we laughed at her throaty chuckle. I wondered why our family was so seldom happy enough to stand together embracing, and why I could not absorb the encircling sweetness but only anticipate the estrangement to come. I felt certain that my going away to school would pull the family further apart. With unutterable shame I realized that I wanted to go anyway. No matter what, I wanted to go.

In February I completed my application. I copied my essays onto the elegant red-and-white form in my best Palmer-method handwriting. My hobbies included water colors and "dramatics," I wrote. ("Hiding behind another personality is a fun carryover from my childhood make-pretend.") I played violin and cello. The most important thing in my life was my family, who supported my decision. One recent experience that was important to me was going out at midnight on Christmas Eve with my father to select a tree. The vendors had closed early on account of the snow, I wrote, so my father had had to climb the fence and throw trees over to me. One year he heaved a dozen before I found one acceptable. Another year the harvest was so plentiful that we packed the car and made deliveries to family and friends. What I didn't say was that we purposely went out after midnight to make sure that the tree-sellers had gone home. Still, it was clearly a case of bald-faced stealing. I wrote as prettily as I could and dared them not to like it.

Chapter Three

In March, my parents received a letter from the Director of
Admissions. St. Paul's School was "pleased," he wrote, to
offer me a place in the class of 1974. For days the letter lay on
the kitchen counter by the telephone. I read it each time I
passed to see again "how much the School wants you to come
here in September."

Once I was accepted, I began to let my schoolmates know
that I'd be going to St. Paul's the next fall. My two closest
girlfriends were the first I had to tell and the hardest. I felt like
a traitor. Not only was I breaking up the threesome—that
didn't matter so much, I figured, since they still had each other,
just as they'd had before they let me into their friendship—but
I was leaving behind girls who were intelligent and loving and
strong. They were my best friends. How was it that I should
have this opportunity and they should not?

The question plagued me all spring. Why not Tyrone Albert,
a smart kid and a football player, as well? He was probably
more what St. Paul's had in mind than I was. They wanted
scholar-athletes, and I couldn't name a sport I was good at.
Why not the kids in my old elementary school in West Philly?
Or my old neighbors, Billy and Rita, for instance, whose mentally ill mother once came across the street wearing nothing but
a bra and a girdle to ask my grandmother for a cigarette.

Billy and Rita were plenty smart. What's more, they were good in ways I didn't even know how to be. Why not them?

During the school day at Yeadon High, I found myself becoming abruptly sentimental. The classmates I had been so ready to leave began to appear clean-cut, all-American. We played jokes on each other, passed notes, giggled. We sneaked candy and miniature water guns up and down our rows of desks. We waved our hands wildly in the air and jumped like babies at any sign of a distraction: *"Ooh, oooh!* Mrs. Hendler, *please!* Aw, me, me! I'll go to the office for you."

Rather than withdraw from the school, I told myself, I should throw myself into it. I sang in the choir. I performed in the school play. In the basement cafeteria Karen and Ruthie and I trained recruits for the majorette squad.

I visited Ruthie, whose big house was divided like a chambered nautilus to accommodate the flow of nineteen children from cradle to move-out. From there the two of us wandered around the corner to Karen's house, where we sat in the dark behind her mother's heavy drapes listening to the Jackson Five and indulging in recreational fault-finding and hair grooming. There were times when we'd sit on the floor saying nothing except whatever wandered into our minds.

"What I want to know is: is that gum on your night table going to get chewed again?"

"Depends."

"On what?"

"On whether either of you have some nice, fresh gum in your pocketbook or whether I have to rely on my already-been-chewed."

"But not overnight!"

"I thought everybody saved theirs."

We bet on who'd stay a virgin the longest, and decided that the last one would buy a bottle of champagne for the other two.

I tried not to think about leaving them, and became numb

with the effort. Spring broke out, new green and flowery, and I missed each wave of bloom. I missed the crocuses and daffodils and the delicate weeping cherries. I caught only nature's neon, the azaleas, as if out of the corner of my eye. Each time I noticed, something had just finished and turned brown.

We corresponded steadily with St. Paul's School that spring about financial aid, room assignment, activities. They suggested clothing for New Hampshire and "questioned the wisdom" of my signing up for six courses instead of the recommended five. (I relented, resentfully.) They advised that I open a checking account with a local bank.

"A checking account!" The cry went up in my family.

"I didn't have a checking account until I was a married woman with a baby!" my mother said.

"Well, honey," said her mother, my grandmother Hamilton, "those children up there start learning about money while we're still bouncing balls."

Nana Hamilton lived in a row house across the street from our old house in West Philadelphia. On the corner, between our two houses, big boys and men played basketball late into the night under the streetlight. When my grandmother, my mother, and my aunts went into the kitchen together, and after my sister and young cousin had fallen asleep, I'd often go upstairs to sit in the dark with my great-grandfather. Pap's skin, crumpled and dry as a paper bag, fit snugly on his skeleton. One gray eye, plagued with glaucoma and cataracts, hung loosely in its sac. He had the bearing of a man who had been bent by age, but not yet neutered or beaten. In his room, I could hear the men's sneakers on the asphalt. I could hear their voices as they teased and cursed each other with gentle violence.

Pap would repeat his stories, old, scary stories from Barbados. When he finished, and I lay listening to the men outside, their voices bouncing off the low ceiling of the city sky, I could hardly visualize St. Paul's. The previous December seemed far away.

Pap and I prayed together on our knees by the sharp metal legs of the open sofa bed:

> A mother's knee, O sacred spot,
> As years go by, forget it not.
> Life could unfold no brighter page
> In youth, in manhood, or in age.
>
> Our father God in faith and love,
> Prepare us for His home above,
> And when we stand before His face
> Let us rejoice, His child of grace.

Outside the men played. I could hear, by the sound of the dribbling, when different players were in control of the ball. Sometimes it nearly sang.

In the glow of the streetlight, I could see Pap talk to His God, an old people's God, One he had turned to, my mother and grandmother joked, after he'd sown his oats but good. Pap's God and his ghosts swirled around him. Death was close in his room; it felt like warm dark and smelled of liniment. I was sad to think of leaving him for St. Paul's, and yet I was grateful for an excuse to escape the seductive stillness of his room.

I was also relieved to escape from my grandmother's glittering fantasies and the heartbreaking remnant of her coloratura soprano; her excess, from the pounds of cheese and butter that bubbled over in her macaroni to her fury; and the madcap humor drinking released in her. I was relieved to imagine myself free of the silent judgment of my dead great-grandmother.

"Grammom would have been so proud of you going to that school," my grandmother said, bestowing on me even greater praise than she could give. "And the wonderful thing is," she added, "that we don't even have to tell you to go up there and make her proud. I know you'll do that already."

When summer came, I worked full time at Woolworth's fountain in Darby. Weeks whizzed by: hot, repetitive, soothing. Each day I wore the same uniform, washed by hand in the sink and hung to dry in the dining room, and the same run-over shoes polished fresh. Each hamburger was cooked the same way; each BLT arranged just so; each soup-to-go poured to the same level in the take-out cup; each basketful of fries allowed to bubble just the same amount of time in their frothy grease. I had it down now. The work felt good.

From her post behind the cash register in John's Bargain Store across Main Street, Karen waved at me through the plate-glass window. "Tacky" Darby passed between us: trolley cars forced to wait while Darbyites double-parked outside the ugly state liquor store; the big white woman in the flowered house-dress who never wore panties (and always bent over); shoplifting teens who met on the sidewalks to compare their heists. Veins raised themselves up along the backs of my hands that summer. My handwriting changed several times. I began reading *Time* magazine.

Soon after that it was time to go.

"I want to talk to you."

I jumped as my mother came upon me in the dark on our front lawn. On the pretext of walking the dog, I had come outside by myself.

"Florence Evans told me that you'd go away, and in my heart I've always known it. I'm not afraid to let you go. Some people say: How could you let her go at fifteen? But I know that if I haven't given you what you need by now, another couple years won't do it. I've done my job. I know that."

I felt a sadness for us at that moment, and for my mother, for whom being a mother was everything. I was desperate to leave her, a desperation that filled me up with shame. I bloated with it. My fingers itched. She looked at my tears with what I imagined to be satisfaction, grim and tender.

Then she came to the point. "I think you know how to behave. I haven't talked to you about how to protect yourself, because you're smart enough to figure that out. You'll do better off staying just as you are. Intact, do you hear me? You're going up there for an education, not for any of that other stuff. Like your cigarettes. I know about girls' feelings, but I'm not about to condone anything. But girls do make mistakes. I know that. And if you ever make a mistake, don't you go running to any of those people up there. You don't know them, and, believe me, they could just be waiting for you to make a mistake. Do you hear me? Don't you go running to those people. If you make a mistake, you come to *me*—not Nana Hamilton, not Nana Jackson, not Aunt Evie, not your girlfriends.

"I have some money. That's just for you to know. It is only for emergencies, but there's enough there if you need it. Do you understand what I'm talking about?"

I nodded.

"Good," she said. "Now, don't stay out here too long."

Getting pregnant, I practically snorted to myself, was out of the question. Not that I couldn't make mistakes. Not that I was judging girls who did. But not me. Not when I had so much to lose.

I thought about being pregnant. I thought about how you

got that way, and my body tingled. It did that not only when I expected it, when a boy held me during a slow dance or kissed me good-night, but at other times too—completely against my will. It did it when Gregory, our paper boy, sang to us girls with exaggerated enjoyment:

> *I'm a girl watcher, I'm a girl watcher,*
> *Watchin' girls go by. My, my, my.*
> *I'm a girl watcher, I'm a girl watcher,*
> *Here comes one now.*

It could jangle despite danger, too. I'd learned that in junior high when two older boys, one black and one white, called out to me after school. They hung out together. That was all I knew about them. They stared at pieces of us girls, at our breasts, our thighs, our buttocks. Once, they asked me to go somewhere with them, and they walked behind me until I'd found a friend to latch onto and accompany home. The clamorous, bulging body under my skin set to jangling with fear, and I spoke about them to my mother.

"Next time they come near you," she said, "I want you to turn around and shout, 'Just what is wrong with you? What is your basic maladjustment?' "

I couldn't say that, of course, so I determined to avoid them. Eventually, they lost interest in teasing me.

Months later, they were arrested, tried, and found guilty of raping and killing a girl in her own basement. She was discovered, as the newspapers said, as my mother often repeated, and as I visualized at odd moments during the school day, in a pool of her own blood.

I remember little else about them or about the incident. It blended into, rather than stood out from, the daily rhythm of my life. It was just like that, adolescence was: jerky, disorderly, the most important times condensed by fear.

I went inside to bed then, because for the first time since I
had applied to St. Paul's School, I realized that I had no idea
what I was getting myself into.

The next morning we left early. St. Paul's fall term began later
than public schools, so my father had to take a day off from
teaching.

Late-model station wagons, weighted down like our Citroën
sedan, drove north with us. We watched them. We counted
them. We took an inventory of their cargo. Suitcases, boxes,
blankets, potted plants, reading lamps; pillows smashed up
against the windows; rocking chairs, easy chairs, rolled up Ori-
entals, and bean bags in various colors lashed to the rooftops
or straddling open back doors. We decided that these folks
were off to college or to boarding schools less stringent than
St. Paul's regarding matters of personal possessions. (The Vice-
Rector had sent us a letter, which my parents approved of,
stating that students were not allowed to own or have access
to automobiles and were strongly discouraged from bringing
expensive objects to school, such as fancy jewelry or stereo
systems.)

I missed my baton. For the first time in three years, I would
not have it close to hand where I could twirl it absently in my
room, to comfort myself with the simple competence of my
fingers and the smooth, cool weight of the metal. I would twirl
at night after my mother had told me to turn off the lights and
stop reading. Even in the morning glare of the Garden State
Parkway I could remember the whirl of silver splinters of light
the baton gave off, and the funnel of air around my head and
legs and behind my back.

St. Paul's did not have majorettes with epaulets and white,
half-calf boots with tassels; it had no cheerleaders, drum ma-
jors, or flag squads; no prom or prom queen; no caps and

gowns at graduation; no class rings such as the big gold one
Wash once gave me and I tried solemnly to give back. I had
the ring, packed up and hidden, but the baton would have
given me away, so I'd left it home with the rest of the folderol
of a public-school education and my gospel choir robes from
church. No sooner were we on the road, however, amid the
station wagons and their cool-eyed passengers, than I missed
each and every public-school artifact.

Three years before, I'd had my hair cut, straightened, and
curled into what had seemed a most sophisticated style. My
mother had warned me that it would have to be maintained:
rolled at night in pink sponge curlers, oiled and brushed and
styled, covered like a matron's in the rain. I agreed happily to
a price I'd never paid. After a few days, when my pressed hair
began to nap up around the temples, when short and sassy
degenerated into short and picky, I tried, one rainy day, to pull
my hair back into a ponytail, as I always had before. The cut
ends wouldn't meet, and, five minutes before the bus was due
on our corner, I stood before our bathroom mirror sobbing
stupidly. What if I had judged that badly again? It was the sort
of blunder I wouldn't know about until too late.

We turned left off Pleasant Street at the sign for the school.
The grounds were green and tidy. At each dormitory house,
parked cars were in various stages of unloading. Young people
called to each other. They darted across lawns and jogged along
the paths; they stood together in groups just as they'd done in
the admissions slides.

My letter said that I was to come directly to the Rectory
where I'd be welcomed by the Rector and my old girl, a Sixth
Former whose job it was to help a new student through the
first confusing days. I remember that we discussed whether to
do that or to go first to my dormitory. We had the map out.

My father drove slowly, but did not stop, and we had some trouble following the pen-and-ink drawing of the campus. Dad kept rolling, and we couldn't decide where we were, which to do first. Eventually, we landed at the Rectory for my official welcome.

The big, gray clapboard Rectory formed a triangle at the center of school with the two red-brick chapels: the homey Old Chapel and the towering Gothic. The brick was repeated in stolid dormitory houses built before the Depression; in low, modern ones that rose in the middle to two-story diamond windows; in the art studios that perched next to a waterfall. White clapboard houses made cheerful spots of light against the grass and trees. An amber-colored system of ponds and streams watered the grounds and enforced a graceful but informal spacing between buildings. From the center greensward to the dining hall or to the meadow behind the Rectory or to the gray granite library, poised like a shrine at the edge of the reflecting pond, we had to cross bridges girded by stone and masonry arches. It was the most beautiful place I'd ever seen, and the most plentiful.

As we headed up the brick walkway toward the Rectory receiving line, I felt a public family face spreading over our countenances. Someone asked us how we'd come up. How long was the drive? Did we drive straight through? Were we tired? Would we like refreshments?

A student runner was dispatched to find my old girl. We were guided into the house by a receiving line of older white students and a few unidentified adults. A black student greeted us, too. His name was Wally Talbot, he told us, and he was president of the Sixth Form. He was a few inches taller than I. He had a smile for the adults that was quick and bright, and a wink for me.

"Did he say that he was president of the School?" my mother whispered.

"I think that's what he said," my father answered, and we all turned around and looked again at the black student who was joking easily with the white students beside him.

The Rector, Mr. Oates, made us a hearty greeting as we walked toward the parlor. He was a smallish man, compact, robust. He looked straight at me and pronounced my name carefully. He looked evenly at my parents, and with respect. He knew where we had driven from, knew that my father had had to take the day off from school. I did not know whether to be flattered or disturbed that a man who'd never seen me knew so much about me and my folks.

We passed through the wide foyer of the Rectory, into an outer parlor and then a large, rectangular living room. My mother and I caught each other taking inventory: fireplaces, bay windows, bookshelves, French doors, rear patio, enclosed porch. Sunlight and birdsong drifted in from gardens. In the outer rooms, more new students arrived with their parents, and more old students greeted them.

I found myself wishing that Mike Russell were there. As Mr. Oates took a moment to exchange some man-talk with my father (they took on the look that men got when they put their hands in their pockets, tilted their heads to one side, and put aside the milder wife-and-kids smiles), I suspected that I had come to this place all on the recommendation of one professionally attentive creature who was now unpacking *his* bags at Harvard. It was the social ease and gentleness that blew so balmy around me that brought Russell to mind. It had been just that confidence that had seduced me, the poise that passed my understanding and made me think that if I were where he'd come from, I, too, would emerge young, gifted, and black for all to admire.

Instead, I stood awkward and ridiculous, cloaked in a makeshift composure so brittle that I seemed fairly to rattle inside it like seeds in a gourd. Instead of Mike Russell, the dashing

Wally with his uptilted eyes and sidelong glances implied a camaraderie I did not feel. Lanky white students made coffee-table conversation. The omniscient Rector, plain-spoken and gray-haired, welcomed us into my new "community." And from where we stood in the Rectory, the green-and-brown grounds spread out around us, pushing the world away, holding me in as if I had been caught in a slide-projector show.

How was I to know (since I could not read Wally's dashing eyes) that other black students had felt the same way? Not until years later was I able to ask them outright and resurrect the strangeness of it all. Ed Shockley, who graduated in my class, can still remember standing outside the Rectory looking at the grounds and wondering whether his white classmates would jump him in the woods.

Lee Bouton, one of the first nineteen girls to arrive at St. Paul's in 1971, came to the Rectory without any family at all. As a tenth-grader, she flew from Washington, D.C., to Boston, caught a bus from Boston to Concord, and then a taxi from Concord to St. Paul's. She carried her own luggage from one transport to the next. It was January when she and the other girls arrived to begin coeducation at St. Paul's. The driver let Lee out in the snow in front of an administration building. The switchboard operator inside called Jeremy Price to come pick up his charge.

Mr. Price "took me to the Rectory, where the welcoming tea was going on. There were parents there, and other students, and I walked through the door with Jeremy Price, feeling very intimidated. He'd taken my bag. I didn't know where my room was. I didn't know anything. And I walked in, and you know how when you walk into that [outer parlor] there's a couch facing the doorway? Well, Loretta [the other black girl] was sitting right in the middle of the couch, and she jumped up and said: 'Ooooooooh! Here's another one!' And she came over and gave me this big hug. And right behind her was Mike Russell with this big, beautiful smile. I felt like, maybe it's going to be all right, you know?''

My family and I stood in the Rectory just a year and a half after Lee's first tea. Unlike her, I was armed with the experience of a proper, on-campus interview, and I was escorted by attractive young parents and a cuddly kid sister. Unlike Ed Shockley, I was not afraid that the white boys were going to catch me alone in the woods one night and beat me up. But for the first time, I had a whiff, as subtle as the scent of the old books that lined the wall, of my utter aloneness in this new world. I reached into myself for the head-to-the-side, hands-on-hips cockiness that had brought me here and found just enough of it to keep me going.

My dormitory was around the corner from the Rectory, over a bridge and across the road from the library. Inside, just off the common room, steps led to the open doorway of the housemaster. He, too, was on hand to greet us.

I wasn't sure about Mr. Hawley. He had a round face whose top half was nearly bald and whose bottom half was covered over with a full, tweed-colored beard. Between the top and bottom halves a pair of glasses perched on a small nose and caught the light. He made a funny face when he spied my sister: "And look what you brought along! We've got a couple of those creatures running around somewhere. I'll see if they've been run over yet by some station wagon gone berserk."

I was later to learn that all the intelligence and will, all the imagination and mischief in that face was revealed in the pale eyes behind the glasses, but on this first meeting, I could only bring myself to concentrate on the beard and the Kriss Kringle mouth.

Mr. Hawley, it turned out, had family in Philadelphia, so we talked about the city, and my parents described for him just exactly where we lived.

Like other St. Paul's buildings, the Hawleys' house had alcoves, staircases, and a courtyard, that presented to me a facade of impenetrable, almost European, privacy. The house-master's home was directly accessible from the dormitory, but only by going from the vestibule into the common room, then up stairs, through a heavy wooden door, into a hallway, and another, inner door. Once in the living room, I could see through the windows that we were across the street from the gray granite library, but I would not have known it had the drapes been pulled. The architecture that I so admired from the outside did not yield itself up to me from within as I had expected. I now felt disconcerted, as I had in the Rectory. Mr. Hawley wanted to know just how far one would drive along Baltimore Pike to get to Yeadon, and I, standing in his living room, had no idea where his kitchen might be.

Mrs. Hawley, a short, soft-spoken woman, appeared from the rear hallway. Like her husband, she said ironic things, but more gently. Startlingly blond children came with her, one peeking from behind her skirt.

Mr. Hawley directed us to my room and showed my father where to park by the back door so that we could unload more handily. We carried my things up from a basement entrance. Doors whooshed open and closed as other girls and their families came and went, and the halls echoed with the sounds of mothers' heels.

My room faced east. In the afternoon it seemed dull and empty and dark.

"This'll be lovely when you get it all fixed up," my mother said, by which I assumed that it looked dull to her, too.

Fine dust had settled contentedly over the sturdy oak bureau and cloudy mirror, over the charming, squat little oak desk and chair and in the corners of the closet. White people, as we said, were not personally fastidious (any black woman who'd ever been a maid could tell you that, and some did, in appalling detail, so I'd heard stories). I was determined to give the place a good wash.

The casement windows matched those elsewhere on campus. My father opened one, tightened the wing nut to hold the sash in place, and stood looking out into the meadow. Then he peeked into the room next door, which was still empty, and recalled how, at Lincoln University, the first students to arrive scavenged the best furniture in the dormitory. "If there's any furniture you don't like, better speak now," he joked. "I guess you wouldn't want to do that here."

I checked the room next door, and pronounced, with laughter but not conviction, that I'd gotten a fair bargain.

The room seemed crowded with all of us about. I found myself chattering on, very gaily, about where I would put my things. What with the windows at one end, the narrow bed against one wall, the bureau, the desk, the radiator, the closet, the door leading into the next room, the door leading in, and the economy of my possessions, there were few options, realistically, for interior design.

Still, I could not stop buzzing. So long as we stood crowded together in the room, my sister jumping on the naked mattress, my mother wondering about smoking a cigarette, my father by the open window clenching his jaw and rubbing the back of his neck, and me burbling and babbling as if words were British soldiers marching in pointless columns, bright and gay, with flags and bright brass buttons on crimson-colored breasts, on and on and on into battle; so long as we had nothing to do except to wait for the next thing to do; so long as the intolerable closeness remained and the intolerable separation loomed to be made, so long would this adrenaline rush through me, anarchic, atavistic, compelling.

Outside the move-in continued. Convinced that I was missing yet another ritual of initiation, I ran down the hall to check the bulletin board. As I stood reading, an Asian boy propelled himself into the vestibule. He introduced himself without smiling and asked me my name. Then, addressing me by the name I gave, he asked whether or not I lived in Simpson House.

"Listen," he said. "There's a girl upstairs. She's just moved in. Her name is Fumiko, and she's from Japan. She can hardly speak any English at all. She understands a lot, but she really needs someone to go and make her feel welcome."

"Do you speak Japanese?"

"Of course not." (He was Chinese-American.) He appeared to be reevaluating me. "Look, is anyone else around?"

"I don't know. I've just arrived myself."

"Well, welcome! Look, we've been helping her, but she needs a girl in her own house, and guys can't come in. Maybe you can tell some of the other girls. Really, she's only just come to the country."

Reluctantly, I agreed. I went to the room on the second floor that the boy had described, and found her. I introduced myself. We tried hard to pronounce each other's names, and we laughed at our mistakes. Fumiko was taller than I. She kept suppressing bows. We agreed to meet again later.

I returned to my family much calmer than I'd left, and I told them about my new friend. Now my mother seemed agitated. Just before we left for dinner, she began to tell me what items of clothing should go into which drawer.

"You always put underwear in the top. See, it's the shallowest one. Big, bulky things like sweaters and jeans go down at the bottom. But, now, please don't just jam your things in. I don't want you walking around here with stuff that's all jerked up."

"I know where things go."

"Listen. Skirts, your good pants, all that stuff needs to be hung up. Let's see how this is packed." My mother unzipped one of the suitcases on the bed. "You know, maybe you might want us to take this big one home. I can't see where you have room to store it."

I watched my mother lift layers of underwear delicately from their berths. Her hands, precise, familiar, called up in me a frenzy of possession. "I've got all night to unpack," I said. "Please don't. I should do that."

"I'll just help you get started. Lord, I hope you don't start putting together any of those crazy outfits you concoct at home. I know you think that stuff looks cute, but it doesn't. You didn't pack any of those fishnet stockings, I hope." Mama selected a drawer for panties and one for bras and slips. I'd brought a girdle—hers, of course—that was hidden in the next layer.

"I *really* want to do that myself."

"I'm not taking anything away from you." Her voice rose with maternal indignation.

"Let the child do it herself," my father said.

I knew that they were going to fight. It would be a silent fight, because we were, even in this room, in public, so long as we were on school grounds. I did not see how we would avoid it. We'd been cooped up together, as my parents called it, all day.

Then my mother laughed. "All right, all right. I was just getting you started," she said. "You'd think I was doing something wrong."

We left for dinner, and I closed my door.

"No locks," my father commented. "I wonder if they ever have any problems."

Outside old students lounged in groups, throwing Frisbees and tossing balls with lacrosse sticks. They halloed one another across the green and complimented new haircuts and tans.

Even the parents knew each other. Mothers in A-line skirts

bent their heads together, and the pastel-colored sleeves of the cardigans they'd thrown over their shoulders flattened against one another like clothes on a rack. Fathers shook hands and laughed in loud voices. At first, they all looked the same to me. People whom we had passed a couple times nodded at us like old acquaintances, and we nodded back with well-prepared poise, although I had no idea whether or not I had spoken to or even seen them before.

As my eyes grew accustomed to the landscape, I noticed different varieties of families. There were fancy white people in big foreign sedans, the women emitting, as I passed near them, a complex cosmetic aroma; there were plain, sturdy people whose hair and nails alike were cut in blunt, straight lines and whose feet were shod in brown leather sandals. Less exotic families emerged from chrome-and-wood station wagons; they wore baggy beige shorts. Almost no one was fat. I could only make out these few gradations, and it unhinged me to know that just a few hours before I had not noticed a one. We ascended the brick pathway to the Upper School building, where meals were served, and we remembered how perilous the walk had been in winter. "Get ready," my parents teased.

After dinner chapel bells announced the First Night Service. Everywhere around us parents were climbing into empty cars and driving away. The air had grown cool. I did not know how to say good-bye to my family. I wanted the leave-taking to be over and my part done right. I wished them gone and was ashamed at the thought. "Please stay," I begged. "Just until chapel's over."

The First Night Service took place, according to tradition, on the first day of each term since the nineteenth century, in the Old Chapel. The Old Chapel was built in the shape of a cross, with smooth rows of wooden pews in the three lower segments and high-backed seats along the walls. The pulpit stood where Christ's head would have hung if he in his gaunt

passion had been nailed to this most charming symbol of suf-
fering. Unlike the grand New Chapel this church was small
and homey. It did not dwarf or intimidate us.

In the Old Chapel my mind flipped through its familiar im-
ages of pious devotion: the Jesus, blond and bland, wispy beard
and wistful eyes, who had smiled at me from over my great-
grandparents' bed, from the Sunday-school room at Ward
A.M.E., from the illuminated cross over the pulpit, and from
cardboard fans and free calendars produced by black funeral
parlors; the brunet Jesus who stretched his arms out toward his
disciples at the Last Supper in my laminated reproduction of
Leonardo da Vinci's oil. *Take, eat.*

The Rector appeared in the pulpit, shorter than he had
seemed in the Rectory, and businesslike. I heard him, despite
the close intimacy of the chapel, as if he were speaking from
far away. Yet even from such a distance, his words—the content of them, if only I could take them out of that solid, white
voice, but I could not quite—had everything to do with me
right then. He talked to us of our fears and our dreams, of our
new career, of the challenges of our life together.

Then he spoke of tradition. Boys had come and gone before
us, sitting in these same pews, thinking and feeling these same
thoughts and feelings. They had grown into men and gone out
into the world prepared, by a St. Paul's education, to do something worthwhile.

My own voices were talking back to him, and so long as he
spoke, I could not control the dialogue. Part of the tradition,
my eye. I was there in spite, despite, *to* spite it. I was there
because of sit-ins and marches and riots. I was there—and this
I felt with extraordinary and bitter certainty—as a sort of
liberal-minded experiment. And, hey, I did not intend to fail.
I remember yawning and yawning, sucking in air with my
mouth closed and my face taut.

Finally, I gave up the effort to pull in his faraway voice. I let myself drift into silence. I watched the old dust settle in the red- and yellow- and blue-tinted sunlight. Above and around the stained-glass windows thick curls of paint peeled away from the walls. Below the windows gold lettering of memorial plaques shone dimly through the dust. A faded semicircle of ornate print above one window reminded us of boys who played in the streets of Jerusalem. In this close, cool chapel, I could not imagine Jerusalem, its noise or its sun. I could not imagine anything. I knew now what they wanted: "No boy shall leave here unimproved."

When the doors opened, I pressed through them into a wash of cool orange twilight. I took off my shoes and was surprised by the wet grass and the freedom to run through it. I ran across grass, asphalt, and brick, past the round post office, the art building, over the bridge. It had been selfish of me to ask them to stay. Daddy would have to drive eight hours tonight. Mom would be tired. Carole had had it. I felt a stitch in my side.

They were waiting at the car. My mother looked at me with dramatic maternity. We were back to baby names, to the familiar fury of the separation I had dreamt of. I heard my sister wail, but I could not see her past my mother. I hugged my mother and my father in the moist air. My cheeks were wet from their kisses. I hugged my sister and felt the panic in her small, perfect body. The soles of my feet throbbed from the bricks.

"Don't stay here in this place," Carole cried. "Aren't you going to come home? You can't stay here!"

My parents got her into the car, and in those days before seat belts, she flailed around in the back seat as I walked my mother to the passenger side. I was sick with my betrayal of Carole and ashamed that I begrudged my parents the thin shreds of devotion I dredged up and flung their way.

I did what I needed to do. I said the things they needed to

hear. I told them that I loved them. I told them that I would miss them. It was true, and it was enough, after all.

They drove away slowly. My mother looked back and waved. My sister cried and cried. I watched her face and waved to it, until it was no more than a speck, until they turned the corner and were gone.

Chapter Four

Still barefoot, I ran into my house to cry. Even when I closed the door to my room, however, I could hear girls. They were talking and laughing. Who could cry? I washed my face and wandered upstairs to Fumiko's room. It was empty. I took the long route back to my room by making a circle down past the common room and peeked in. Two black students, a boy and a girl, smiled back at me.

Jimmy Hill, one of the skinniest boys I had ever seen, had arrived that morning from Brooklyn. He had extravagant brown eyes. His black satin jacket, emblazoned on the back with a red-and-yellow dragon, hung open to reveal a fishnet T-shirt that cast tiny shadows on his chest.

Annette Frazier was a ninth grader (or "Third Former," as I was learning to say) whose theatrical mannerisms made her seem older than she was. She had an appealing face, rounded, with regular features that she used to great effect. When we met, she pantomimed our wariness with a quick movement of her eyes. She caught precisely our exposure and our collusion.

We shouted with laughter and touched hands. Had anyone told me two hours before that I would be engaging in such high-decibel, bare-naked black bonding, I would have rolled my eyes with scorn. We sat in our small circle until Annette decided that it was time for her to get back to unpacking her things. I wondered if she was as organized and as self-assured as she looked. Neither Jimmy nor I could face our rooms, so we left together in search of a place to smoke.

We found one next to the squash courts. It was marked by a sand-filled stone urn and a few butts. We liked the place, because we could smoke there, and because we had a solid wall to lean on and buildings with which to swaddle ourselves against the open sky.

I was not afraid to go to St. Paul's School, although it was becoming clear to me from the solicitous white faces that people thought I was—or ought to be. I had no idea that wealth and privilege could confer real advantages beyond the obvious ones sprawled before us. Instead, I believed that rich white people were like poodles: overbred, inbred, degenerate. All the coddling and permissiveness would have a bad effect, I figured, now that they were up against those of us who'd lived a real life in the real world.

I knew that from a black perspective Yeadon had been plenty cushy, but after all, I had been a transplant. West Philly had spawned me, and I was loyal to it. Jimmy felt just as unafraid, just as certain as Darwin that we would overcome. Jimmy had grown up in the projects, the son of a steadfast father and a mother who was a doer, a mover who led tenant-action and community groups. Together, his parents had raised a boy who had a job to do.

"Listen to me, darling," he said. "We are going to turn this motherfucker out!"

And why not? I, too, had been raised for it. My mother and her mother, who had worked in a factory, and her mother, who had cleaned apartments in Manhattan, had been studying these people all their lives in preparation for this moment. And I had studied them. I had studied my mother as she turned out elementary schools and department stores.

I always saw it coming. Some white department-store manager would look at my mother and see no more than a modestly dressed young black woman making a tiresome complaint. He'd use that tone of voice they used when they had *important* work elsewhere. Uh-oh. Then he'd dismiss her with his eyes. I'd feel her body stiffen next to me, and I'd know that he'd set her off.

"Excuse me," she'd say. "I don't think you understand what I'm trying to say to you . . ."

And then it began in earnest, the turning out. She never moved back. It didn't matter how many people were in line. It didn't matter how many telephones were ringing. She never moved back, only forward, her body leaning over counters and desk tops, her fingers wrapped around the offending item or document, her face getting closer and closer. Sometimes she'd talk through her teeth, her lips moving double time to bite out the consonants. Then she'd get personal. "How dare you," would figure in. "How dare you sit there and tell me . . . " Finally, when she'd made the offense clear, clearer even than the original billing error or the shoddy seam, she'd screw up her eyes: "Do you hear me? Do you hear what I'm saying to you?"

They'd eventually, inevitably, take back the faulty item or credit her charge or offer her some higher-priced substitute ("like they should've done in the first place," she'd say, and say to them). They would do it because she had made up her mind that they would. Turning out, I learned, was not a matter of style; cold indignation worked as well as hot fury. Turning out had to do with will. I came to regard my mother's will as a force of nature, an example of and a metaphor for black power and black duty. *My* duty was to compete in St. Paul's classrooms. I had no option but to succeed and no doubt that I could will my success.

Jimmy understood. He knew the desperate mandate, the uncompromising demands, and the wild, perfect, greedy hope of it. If we could succeed here—earn high marks, respect, awards; learn these people, study them, be in their world but not of it—we would fulfill the prayers of our ancestors. Jimmy knew as I did that we could give no rational answer to white schoolmates and parents who asked how we had managed to get to St. Paul's School. How we got there, how we found our way to their secret hideout, was not the point. The point was that we had been bred for it just as surely as they. The point was that we were there to turn it out.

When I got back to my house, I concentrated on learning names. Alison, Ruthie, Sara. Those were the first I picked up, because they were the old girls, the most assured and welcoming. They told me where the storeroom was, how many coins the washer and dryer required. They told me that there was an iron and ironing board upstairs, and a hot plate. They told me that another master—a woman—lived just above me in a tiny apartment.

They also asked questions. Where was I from? Who did I know? Had we driven? Take long? What Form was I in? What classes? Everyone asked and answered the same queries as if there were nothing else in the world to talk about. And, yet, I had nothing else to say, either. Helplessly, I answered their questions and asked the same questions back.

So it went while I unpacked until Pam Hudson moved into the room adjoining mine. She was a new Fifth Former, too. She used her husky voice to curse liberally as she shoved handfuls of clothes into drawers. She was more delicate in her handling of her stereo and guitar.

Pam wanted to know whether I felt as "weird" in this new place as she did. She wanted to know if I was scared, whether I smoked, what I liked to eat.

She looked in a few times while I cleaned. I washed and

waxed my linoleum floor, re-creating in myself the anxious thrill of my mother's housecleaning. I hummed to myself as I scrubbed the tiny space. *What can wash me white as snow? Nothin' but the blood of Jesus.*

I closed my door so that the girls would not see me on my knees or hear me hum. Pam Hudson saw, but I didn't mind. It calmed me to hear her on the other side of the half-open door just as it calmed me to rub a rag in circles across the floor.

"I can't believe you're doing that," Pam said.

"Shhh," I said to her when I finished. "Now I am going to sit here in the middle of the bed and let my nice, clean room seep into me."

"You're nuts."

I laughed with her as if I had been joking. But when she closed the door, I waited for the onset of the brittle serenity I had sought. The Westminster chimes pealed and crickets chirped, but peace did not descend, and time did not slow down. I had not wiped away fear and the chaos it could bring. I went upstairs to find Fumiko to see if I couldn't be of some use and find a friend to bind to me.

I awoke the next morning to birdsong from the meadow. The bathroom was a different story. Fluorescent light splashed off the mirrors; metal stall doors banged, toilets flushed, showers sprayed full blast. A window was open to clear the steamy air. In rushed the roar of the waterfall below.

Having grown up with bathtubs, I hated showers, but I took one. When I opened the curtain to reach for my towel, I saw that a girl was waiting to take my place. She started for the stall as I stepped out for my towel, effectively barring my path back to where I had intended to dry myself. A geyser of anger shot up inside me and subsided. Next time I would not leave my towel so far from the stall.

The ablutions were not complete. I had yet to brush my teeth, but I'd left the toothbrush and toothpaste in my room. I had to comb my hair, but those implements, too, were in my room. I started out of the bathroom for the toothbrush, but had not finished drying, and before I could dry, I had to put my soap down. By now, the sinks were crowded with spitting, face-washing, hair-combing girls, some groggy, some chatty and refreshed. I tried to find space to rest my soap. It slipped. When I picked it up it was fuzzy with dust and hair.

By the time I dressed I felt as if I had been awake a long time. I trucked to the Upper with girls from Simpson. In the dining room, a group of black students motioned me to join them. A boy was describing school dances:

"First they turn the music up as high as it will go. It's blaring and blasting and some white boy calls himself singing, and he's screaming and hollering. Then they all come in and start jumping up and down—" he jerked his body around in his seat, "and they're just *it*. 'Oh, wow, isn't this neat? Oh, man, this is so fun! Oh, super!'

"It's terrible. No, really, don't laugh, it's a shame. Naw, I'm serious. I feel sorry to see people carrying on like that." He opened his mouth wide and threw his head back. We, his audience, laughed with him.

Alma, the girl who had talked to us on the path last winter, bounced out of her seat to take her plate to the kitchen for second helpings. Alma had arrived late from Memphis the day before. She'd come into the cafeteria wearing dark pants and a white sailor's blouse. The night before, as at breakfast, she had been back for more. I envied her the unashamed gusto that only the slender could bring to a meal.

I went to the kitchen for coffee, and asked, having already

learned the lunchroom etiquette, if anyone wanted me to bring
something back for them. For the first time, someone made a
request. It was my second meal on my own, and that request
felt like belonging.

We walked to chapel in a bunch, five abreast on the pathway. We talked and laughed loudly and wrapped ourselves in
the sound of our own voices and the mass of bodies in the
group. Some of the boys wrestled as we went. By the time our
unruly company mounted the steps to the Chapel terrace, the
three-minute bell rang above our heads. I had just enough time
to find my assigned seat.

When the organist concluded the prelude, a voice directing
us to rise and sing the appointed hymn emerged from speakers
above our heads. For twenty minutes students and teachers
coughed and sneezed, listened, and daydreamed together as the
Rector spoke. We sang another hymn, and the organ erupted
into life again. Students sprang out of their seats only to shuffle
in the press for the door. Older masters laid their heads back
against the wall and listened to the organ. Outside we formed
a semicircle around the Chapel door. The Rector stood above
us on the top step and, when we had assembled, read the day's
announcements:

The day's classes would be held according to a special, short-
ened schedule: consult your computer-printed class rosters. Students who had not received their rosters should report to the
Registrar's office immediately. Post-office-box combinations
would be given out at the following times. Athletic schedules
would be posted on the athletic bulletin board on the first floor
in the Schoolhouse. Lockers would be assigned that afternoon.

There were times and places given for changing classes, directions for questioning room assignments, lists posted for assigned tables at Seated Meal, to which boys were told to wear
jackets and ties and girls to wear dresses, appropriate skirts
and blouses, or pants suits. (The pants-suits directive, one that

brought to mind the polyester knits that were all the rage with my mother's and grandmother's friends, had been a small victory for girls the year before. Originally, they had been allowed to wear only dresses. They had been very cold that first winter.)

Teenage intuition told me that it would be uncool to take notes during announcements, but halfway through, I gave in and began scribbling. Mr. Oates finished reading and dismissed us with a smile. The student body turned and snaked its way toward the Schoolhouse. We "newbs," as new boys were called (and new girls, too, for the time being), clutched our schedules. The lower formers, little seventh- and eighth-grade boys, bobbed about in clumps, no taller than my shoulder, of three to five. Older students strolled by us displaying their self-assurance ostentatiously.

My teachers were all men. There was Sr. Fuster, who spoke in Spanish to old and new students alike. He even cracked Spanish jokes, and punctuated them with sight gags for those of us who couldn't follow the language fast enough to catch the humor. Mr. Buxton, our athletic English teacher, gave us a syllabus and outlined our course. He was clear, blunt, organized. In an effort to keep from gawking, I frowned a lot as he spoke. Our math teacher, Mr. Clark, was a tall, lanky man whose age I could not determine. He seemed to have been at St. Paul's during "The War," but I wasn't sure which one. He liked to laugh and made a yuk-yuk sound in his throat that bobbed his Adam's apple.

Now the maleness of the school impressed itself on me. In each class of ten or twelve only three or four of us were girls. Men's and boys' voices reverberated in the buildings. Their shoulders bumped against me coming into class. Their legs and feet stretched out as if by divine right under the table, and their big arms and fingers on top. Some talked over us as a matter of course; others were pointedly deferential. I remember being glad that I wasn't one of the white girls. Boys stared at them. I watched them looking from one to the other and then back again to one particular girl or some part of her: her hair, her arm, the nape of her neck.

That morning I also attended my first religion class. I resented the requirement. The African Methodist Episcopal Church had given me an "Introduction to Christianity." Besides, Intro was a year-long course, and, as a Fifth Former, I had little enough time to sample the good courses listed in the catalog: modern dance, Southeast Asia, black American literature and history, woodworking, astronomy . . . In fact, as we settled into our chairs around the big table, I laughed inwardly, recalling how, the day before, I had told a master, whose name I could not remember, just what I'd thought about force-fed sacred studies. Not much.

At the buzzer a man with heavy features and dark hair threw open the door and looked around. His eyes sparkled with mischief when he looked at me.

"Good morning," he said. "My name is Reverend Ingersoll. I happen to know that some of you are not looking forward to the course. One person here even told me that this class looked like it was going to be a complete waste of time."

My classmates loved it. They laughed and slapped each other's hands. My ears felt hot.

"I hope that that person will not feel that way by the end of the course. This is not so much religious instruction as it is an exploration of our spiritual lives. What does it mean to be human? Who am I? Why am I here? What is the meaning of life?

"Your first assignment is to read the first four pages of *Dynamics of Faith*," he held up a slim volume to general moaning, "by Paul Tillich. It is available in the bookstore."

"Just four pages?" one boy asked.

"Just four."

.   .   .

Faith is the state of being ultimately concerned: the dynamics of faith are the dynamics of man's ultimate concern. Man, like every living being, is concerned about many things, above all those which condition his very existence, such as food and shelter. But man, in contrast to other beings, has spiritual concerns—cognitive, aesthetic, social, political. Some of them are urgent, often extremely urgent, and each of them as well as the vital concerns can claim ultimacy for a human life or the life of a social group. If it claims ultimacy it demands the total surrender of him who accepts this claim, and it promises total fulfillment even if all other claims have to be subjected to it or rejected in its name. . . .

"Don't read me any more of that, darling. Please, *please* don't read any more. You're frying my brains." Jimmy put his hand over the page.

"Can you believe this?" I asked him.

"Here, have another cigarette."

"I can't smoke up any more of yours."

"Get outta here. I got a whole carton in my room. Here, smoke. *Smoke!* Anybody who's got to read more of that shit deserves a cigarette."

"Did I tell you about how he looked at me when he walked in? I could have died."

"I wish I could have seen it. Well, if you didn't die then, that Tillich stuff will kill you for sure."

"Don't joke about it. To you it's a joke. To me, it's for real."

"All I can say is that I'm glad I'm not a Fifth Former. I'd hate to come in and have to face that—" he pointed to the skinny paperback whose first four pages were curled back. "What are they trying to prove?"

"They're trying to be hard. It's like: You think you're smart? Check this out. But I've *got* to understand it."

"OK, start with the title. What's the title?"

"*Dynamics of Faith.* What's a dynamic?"

"Beats the hell out of me."

I wanted to talk more about religion, but Jimmy was bored. "What sport are you taking?" I asked him.

"Cross-country."

"Don't do that, Jimmy."

"Well, what else am I going to take? Look at me. Look at me! What else am I going to play, football?

"Go ahead, laugh," he said. "It is laughable. I know it. That's why I'ma stay the hell away from it. Or soccer? Have you ever seen them play soccer?"

"I'm taking soccer."

"You go ahead. You'll do fine. I know it. But I do not want anybody busting me down in some mud after a ball. Cross-country'll be fun. Nice little run through the woods . . ."

"You know what they'll do to you, don't you? I heard that they run you into the ground. I heard they run you until you puke in the snow."

"That's not cross-country, that's lacrosse. Besides, there's no snow yet. I wish they had wall-ball, 'cept I guess that's not really a sport."

Fumiko met me on the way to soccer.

"Do you play basketball?" she wanted to know.

"Nah." I felt rough in her presence, square-fingered, and loud.

"I like basketball. In Japan, I played a *lot* of basketball. Don't you play at all?"

"A little bit. I don't shoot so well."

"I can teach you! It's easy. I'll teach you." She looked at her watch. "Come on. We have time."

In the gymnasium we heard the commotion below in the locker rooms. Fumiko ran to the wall behind the basket where a few balls lay beside each other. She picked one, dribbled it, and then passed it to me. She ran onto the court, and I passed it back to her. She shot the ball. It headed toward the basket in a low arc and dropped through. She ran hard to retrieve her own rebound. There could have been four girls after her, as hard as she ran. She snatched the ball out of the air and then leapt to make a lay-up. It hit the backboard softly and fell through the hoop. Then she passed me the ball.

I hesitated and passed it back. She thrust it at me. I caught the pass, chest-high. She threw it as perfectly as a diagram, harder than my old gym teacher, and with no effort I could see.

I did not want to play. I wanted to watch. But she seemed intent on teaching me. Her intelligence and force were as obvious as her athleticism. I had seen none of it before, because I'd been so eager to assume her need for me.

"Hold like this," Fumiko said. She stood behind me in order to position not just my fingers but my arms as well. She pushed me with her body. I was confused. Her language had been so delicate that I hadn't expected the shove.

I shot. The ball bounced off the rim.

"Hah!" Fumiko zoomed down the key for the rebound and rocketed another pass to me. I caught it. My palms tingled. This time she told me to dribble to the basket. She followed me close. Her body was so close and new that I dropped the ball. She laughed.

Out of the corner of my eye I watched her as we walked to soccer practice. "You are really good." I felt ashamed for having thought of her as a geisha girl. I had done to her what I suspected white people did to me. She did not answer me. I did not repeat myself. It would've been too much like amazement; after all, the girl had told me that she could play.

Green fields stretched out before us. Two soccer fields lay end to end. A line of white paint on the grass divided them, and the four goals lined up like giant white wickets. Beyond them were clay tennis courts and a gravel track. Football fields hid behind a stand of trees at the end of the track. Big and small boys ran past us toward the far fields. Fumiko broke into a run, too, and I trotted along. By the time we got there, I was out of breath.

We flung ourselves onto the damp grass to lounge in the sun with the other girls.

"Have you people finished your laps already?" The voice behind us was blunt, the pronunciation lippy and controlled. Miss Breiner, the modern-languages teacher, appeared in pastel-colored shorts and knee socks. She was one of the few women at the school who wore makeup. "Four laps. Four laps, please, so we can get started."

I could not help but stare at the field. It was as big around as a Philadelphia city block. I knew people who would get in their cars and *drive* that far. The other girls groaned dramatically and started running. I couldn't do it. I'd die.

"Excuse me, Miss Breiner," I said. This would look like shirking, I knew. Her powder-blue eyes studied a clipboard.

"Yes," she said without looking up.

"My parents wrote to the school this summer to tell them that I have asthma."

"I see," she said looking at me. "I know a couple other girls here who have asthma. Do you take medication? Do you have pills?"

Behind me I heard the thunder of distant cleats. "No." I didn't know there *were* pills for asthma. "But I use an inhaler when I need to."

Miss Breiner was finished regarding me. I could see myself in those blue eyes: a robust black girl talking about asthma and didn't even have pills. "Do what you can," she said. "You may find that the exercise will actually help your asthma."

I fell in. What had started as a pack stretched into a column nearly a quarter lap long. Ahead of me girls talked to each other as they ran. One sprinted to sneak up behind another and give her ponytail a yank. Ponytails flashed in the sun. Striding legs stretched out before me like a movie. My breath came so fast now that I had to concentrate as if to break through some partition stretched across my lungs. It had to be some failing of mine. I was breathing too fast, that was it. I'd slow it down and let the air go deeper. But then I began to wheeze, and the long, lithe girls in front of me were coming up behind me now, passing me. How had I dropped so far behind? I pumped my legs as hard as I could.

"Do not cut corners. Do not cut corners." Miss Breiner's voice caught me out. She'd be watching me now, for sure.

My arms flailed. I'd never run so far in my life. What were those pills? The top of my body swung from side to side, and none of it, the pumping or flailing or desperate prayer, pushed me forward.

When everyone else finished, I slunk into the huffing group. I was gulping at the air. It came into my lungs in teaspoonsful. One girl asked me if I was all right. I nodded. It cost too much air to talk.

Then practice began. We passed and kicked and chased the ball. It changed direction in an instant. It was tyrannical, capricious. At the end of practice we did little sprints. Fumiko won most of them. After practice she grinned at me. Her face was flushed and happy.

"I can't do this every day, Fumiko," I said as we walked to Simpson.

In my room I sat on the bed and sucked at my inhaler. The medicine spread through my chest like warmth blown in through tiny copper wires. I thought hard about how to handle this soccer business, and decided to get to practice early in order to do laps before Miss Breiner appeared. After two slow ones, I could quit without being suspected—and still have

time to get my wind back before practice. I rationed my cigarettes (but I didn't quit), and lobbied for the position of
goalie.

About forty minutes was allotted in the community schedule
for bathing and dressing before class at 5:15. At first, eighth-
period class seemed cruel and redundant. We carried with us
the fatigue of the day but also, much as I hated to admit it,
the weary refreshment of exercise. Our teachers, tired from their
own classes and sports, seemed less critical and demanding. I
felt less competitive. I had made it through another day, and
dinner was imminent. Night was coming, and the dark pushed
us closer together.

When I did not have an eighth-period class I would meander
back to my room to inhale my medicine and drift into a short,
light sleep. St. Paul's was not yet integrated into my dreams.
At six o'clock I awoke to Pam Hudson's folk music. It was
time to dress for dinner.

Four days a week we sat at assigned tables, one master (and
sometimes a spouse) and six or seven students at each one. At
six-thirty the head of the dining hall asked the Lord to "Bless
this food to our use and us to thy service." Student waiters
piled into the kitchen with their empty trays and emerged carrying the evening meal in serving bowls. The faculty served us,
talked to us, and asked questions of us as we ate, so that each
table acquired the personality of its master. Seating changed
every three weeks. Despite the rudimentary etiquette (we did
not eat until everyone at table was served; we tried to ask for
seconds rather than grab for them; and we did not ask to be
excused until dessert was served), we ate fast. Most of us gobbled our bread and washed it down—someone was always being dispatched for more pitchers of milk and water—to hold
us until the waiter arrived. Then, after the master dished up
plates, we bolted the main meal while somebody dashed to the

kitchen for seconds. Young boys ate the most and with the least complaint. We older girls were duty-bound to eat least. I tried to pick and fuss like the skinny girls, but I gave up; I was hungry and tired by dinnertime; I was freshly scrubbed and wearing a clean dress and a smear of lip gloss. If I did not eat my fill I'd be ready to cry by bedtime. So I chowed down with the boys. I helped clear our plates (no stacking on the tables), and devoured dessert. By the end of Seated Meal, the heavy food for young boys in a cold climate thudded to the bottom of my belly, and my sense of well-being was restored as simply as a child's. Then I could observe my new schoolmates.

In the three dining rooms, a few tables crowded round, after the assigned diners had been excused, with students who wanted an audience with particular teachers. Debaters joined intellectuals and a few lonely hearts to assemble around Mr. Katzenbach, a man as corpulent as he was articulate. I heard that he had a law degree, and that he was "brilliant." Even at his most casual, he was passionate, eclectic, witty. The students around him spoke grammatically and vehemently, and studied his face for approval as they talked.

Sr. Fuster attracted a loose, motley group. Some Spanish Club business took place, but mostly, they kept company. He held the boys by the backs of their necks and patted the girls' hands with his manicured fingers. They called him Fu-Fu.

Other groups hung on in the dining rooms around other teachers: athletes with favorite coaches, girls with women, clubs and societies with their advisers. Eventually, though, many crowded into discernible cliques in the smoke-filled common room. (The Rector would later astound us with the information that only a few dozen students had actually secured from their parents the letter granting them permission to smoke. The common room in those days teemed with unauthorized smokers who, like me, felt safe in the crowd. In 1988 smoking was banned altogether, as it had been until 1971.) Each group pulled around itself a membrane to shield itself from the others. Some of the membranes were more permeable than others.

One group that attracted my attention was the artsy sophisticates. The girls wore low-cut black dresses, bosoms white and plump as the Renaissance. The boys, too, were pale, languid, bored. They appeared the most self-possessed, but studied, of the groups.

A Greenwich, Connecticut, crowd, held together by nothing more than short hair and a fondness for corduroy, as far as I could see, was just as cohesive. There was a tiny super-rich, European-traveling set and their entertaining hangers-on; a pimply, giggly group of hairless boys who played computer games and wore their pants too short; a small group of freaks, whose hair hung longer, whose pants were slung lower over their protruding hipbones, and whose cynicism, though less articulate, ran deeper than others'. Conspicuously absent were the lower formers, seventh- and eighth-grade boys who were due back in their dormitories for prescribed study times, and who were, in any event, too young and scared to make after-dinner small talk. They traveled back to their houses in chest-high clumps and slept in wards where their beds were separated only by curtains. In the far corner were the black and Hispanic kids, whose base was a blue couch and battered coffee table.

Our corner admitted others, white scholarship kids from Concord who came to see that they had at least as much in common with us as with anyone else, social radicals, foreign students who had not yet found a clique. (Fumiko told me later that she fell in with us because at first ours were the only faces that she could readily distinguish one from another.) And from our blue couch, we allowed each other to roam to other groups: José Maldonado could choose to huddle with his hulking football and lacrosse pals; Steve Isaac with his ice hockey chums; Anthony Wade with the science buffs. (A couple of black kids never came to the blue couch, never spoke to us at all, because they clearly wanted to assimilate. We shunned them back. They appeared not to notice.)

I wanted to know to what extent the group dictated its members' movement, to what extent it presumed to dictate mine. St. Paul's School, which I had imagined would liberate me from the tyranny of home life, had me confined in a rigid regimen of chapel, classes, sports, mealtimes, activities, meetings, homework. Nobody here would say, "When I say jump, you supposed to ask, how high?" But that was surely how it felt. I could not buck the school, but I was damned if I was going to let my own black peers boss me around, too. The first Third World Coalition meeting did nothing to assuage my defiance.

We held the meeting in the common room of the squash courts under photos of the first high school squash teams—St. Paul's own—in the country. The officers sat at a round table in the front of the room. The rest of us lounged on sturdy captain's chairs and love seats the color of a cloudy day. Originally, the group had been named the Afro-Am. It had commanded its own room for meetings, recreation, and dances. That had been under the reign of Bernard Cash, the president who had graduated the previous spring.

It was Cash who had led the group to power, I learned, Cash who had defied the administration, Cash who had spurred the group to press for black books in the curriculum and respect for the black presence in the school, Cash who'd helped lead the coat-and-tie rebellion before coeducation. The boys who were now our leaders seemed to assume that those days were over, that we here were living in a lesser time.

I felt no loyalty to Cash. I had seen him once, at my interview. I had seen his photos in our pamphlets. I knew the attitude, the cocked head, the gold-rimmed shades, the hat, or, when he chose to go bare-headed, the Afro with the off-center part that looked as if it had been made with a hatchet. He had been bigger and meaner than I could ever be, as big and as black as I supposed white people expected, or hoped; and the line of succession that descended from him was as male as the apostles. I bristled at the mention of his name, and yet, I wanted to know more.

Mr. Price came in late and sat in the corner. He listened impatiently to the discussion about the season's first bash. Then we new students were welcomed with a warning from the old boys: the coming years would be hard, they said, and we'd need to lean on them. That's how they had made it through—just barely, someone joked—and that's how we would survive. Mr. Price allowed as how he, too, was available for help, and one of the officers, laughing, apologized for the omission. Lack of respect for him mingled with camaraderie.

The younger new students seemed to be listening appreciatively. I liked their looks, but scorned their fervent desire to belong. Here we were alone, together, and passing along to each other the very same message I had gotten elsewhere. I hadn't come to St. Paul's to *survive,* I had come to turn it out, and who were they to tell me I couldn't do it, couldn't expect to do it, couldn't even hope?

"Well, and good, we have the bash settled, but can we talk about a purpose for the year now? Some goals to achieve? I mean, it's nice to have the social stuff or whatever. Hey, I like a bash as much as the next guy, but we are a political group." It was Ed Shockley. Even sitting, he towered over the rest of us. His face was triangular and scowling. "We were, at least. I assume that we still are. Aren't we?"

"Well, sure," Maldonado said. "You got any ideas?"

"Well, there's lots of things. I can think of a dozen, but it's supposed to come from the group. That's what we're here for."

The banter was playful, but sharp. I could not figure out who was disciplining whom.

"I think we should continue the kind of things we started with Cash and them," Ed said. "This community has the feeling that everything's just fine, and it's not, and we need to keep saying that, by any means possible."

"We could do another play," said a fat girl named Sharon. (I had already heard the boys making jokes about her size.)

Addie, who sat next to her, shouted with enthusiasm: "Oh, a play! That was great last year!"

Some of the boys mimicked her. "A play! A play!"

"Come on, you guys. The sister's got an idea. Let's have some respect. No need to be trifling about it." Maldonado had the stature to scold and the ability to do it gently.

Mr. Price cleared his throat and delivered a short lecture. We needed, he said, to put as much energy into our studies as we seemed willing to put into dancing or social reform. Nobody would listen to anything we had to say if our grades weren't solid. With half as much effort put into math as basketball, we'd find our minds clearer and more able to figure out what we could do to change St. Paul's. There was a whole host of ideas—not just what others had done before, but new tactics for new challenges—that we were nowhere near to discovering. If we weren't academically viable, we'd never be politically credible.

Then he left.

"Well, damn!"

"Like, would it kill him to tell us some of these wonderful ideas of his?"

"He doesn't have any ideas. He just wants people to feel bad."

"The man's right. I hate the motherfucker's guts, but he's right."

"If he's so right, then how come he can't show some 'academic excellence' in his own class?"

Kenny Williams, another Philadelphian, pulled his face into a scowl to mock Mr. Price: " 'Ah, any questions, comments?' "

We laughed uproariously. "Questions, comments." In a minute everyone was saying it.

"Nah, really," said Kenny, who had been quiet, "if Mr. Price came prepared to class, hey, that'd go a long way to improving the black curriculum."

"Thing that makes me mad is that when he's in the mood, the man can deliver the goods."

"Get up and walk out. I suppose that's excellence."

"You know that really is unfair." Carmen spoke up. She was a brown-skinned Hispanic girl who lived on my floor, a devoted dancer who would begin stretching at odd moments. Hers was a bodacious, African body, small at the top and as full and firm as a fertility goddess in the back. She exuded a flamboyant hauteur.

Carmen snorted a little, as she frequently did, before she continued. "I mean, honestly. Mr. Price may come down hard sometimes, but that's only because he cares. Who else around this place takes the time to come to our meetings? Who else goes to talk to our teachers when we're having problems? And lest some of us forget, who else is willing to go to the financial-aid officer when we run out of money? Hmmmm? I mean, honestly."

There was humor in the haughty bearing, and the group granted Carmen her point, although not without comment.

"Right, and who else came into the Afro-Am room and tore the place up? Who else threw a chair at Ed?"

"C'mon, Carmen, you know that's your boy."

"You're the only one he likes."

"I am not."

"If he brought me presents from Boston, I'd be his boy, too."

"All right, all right," José said. "I'm inspired. Who's going to work on coming up with a play?"

"And we should do a chapel presentation. At least one during the fall."

"OK. Who's going to work on that? You work on it. It was your idea. So, you don't want to work, keep your mouth shut.

"Seriously. The first order of business is the chapel presentation. We got the idea from people over here in this corner. Stay after the meeting if you want to work with them. Then what? You guys'll have a report for us at the next meeting, tell us what the chapel program will be? OK. Done. Great. Come on, you guys, the pizza man cometh."

A Concord take-out shop delivered pizzas every night at nine-thirty. It explained why football players passed up seconds of baked fish. I wondered where brothers got the money.

"And to all of you new people," someone added, "you don't *have* to mess around for a year before you get it right. In fact, it'd be easier to start off right now! Any problems, just grab somebody."

When the meeting ended, a boy named Sam introduced himself. "Aw, come on, Oobs," the boys said as they passed us. "Don't try to rap. You know you can't rap, man."

"Isn't it our job to welcome new students?"

"Yeah, right."

"So, how did you like your first Third World meeting?"

I wanted to shout at him, because he seemed safe to shout at, because I didn't know if this was a rap or merely a friendly greeting, because I thought that somehow he whom the other boys teased so mercilessly, might understand. I did not shout. Instead, my voice in the thin night air sounded peevish.

"I didn't expect that there'd be such a big deal about parties.

And I certainly didn't think that there'd have to be a debate about our being political. I mean having parties is fine, but really, don't people want to do something else?"

"Sure, and we will. You should have been here when Cash was here."

"I hate to say it, but I'm really tired of hearing about Cash."

"He was amazing. It's probably hard for you, because you never knew him, but he was . . . well, you had to be there. I know that sounds crazy, but the man was really something. He had charisma. He was powerful. I mean, white people listened to him, to us."

I had heard from one of the girls that three guys had once stolen into Sam's room and urinated into his bureau drawer. I wondered if it was true. I wondered if Cash had been one of them.

How was I to know then, as I learned years later, that Cash, too, felt alone behind his shades? How could I have guessed that that loneliness seared him inside his own skin like salt, and the rest of us, too?

"I was as isolated from Negroes as I was from whites," James Baldwin wrote (in a book lent to me by Mr. Lederer, a Jewish teacher at St. Paul's), "which is what happens when a Negro begins, at bottom, to believe what white people say about him."

What did these white people say in a hundred ways but that we were somehow different from the common run of black people out there in America? What did they say but that we were special, picked out for a special destiny? I was ashamed even to consider the possibility, but it was hard not to believe sometimes. How could I know that my special aloneness united me with my peers more surely than the wary, competitive fraternity I tried to create in my own heart?

How could I guess that Bernard Cash had once been, as he calls himself, a black nerd, like the rest of us, stalking through the projects of White Plains with big feet and thick glasses, trying to escape drug-dealers who littered the landscape like broken wine bottles, self-hatred as seamless as skin? How was I to suspect that he was the baby of his family; or that his mother mailed boxes of peanut butter and bread to him in Concord, because she was used to leaving a sandwich wrapped in waxed paper for him to comfort himself with when he awoke, as he always did, in the middle of the night?

I had learned from repetition:

Just like a nigger.

Nothin' worse than a sorry nigger.

Problem is, we don't strive for nothing. We satisfied with any old thing.

I don't know why them Muslims need to wear them rags on their heads; don't we look bad enough already?

We don't take care of our own.

We don't learn.

We don't apply ourselves.

That's some sure enough niggershit going on there.

I hate to say it, but you know these niggers ain't shit. Don't you grow up like these do-nothing Negroes around here.

What is wrong with us? What is wrong with us? What is wrong with us? Can you tell me what is wrong with my people?

I just don't know why we can't do right. . . .

I learned through repetition, and I carried with me what I learned.

> *Niggers and flies I do despise;*
> *The more I see niggers,*
> *The more I like flies.*

It jangled as noisily in my head as the hormones in my body. And what with all the racket, how could I have hoped to listen to the longings of my peers and know they were my own? How could I have imagined the crinkling of Cash's waxed paper in the dark?

Chapter Five

Early in my first term at St. Paul's I began to dream old dreams. They were childhood dreams that I had thought I'd done with, like bed-wetting. In one dream, I was encircled by bears, friendly, round-faced teddies as big as I. The bears were animated, sepia-colored versions of pen-and-ink drawings in one of my books. In the dream I was a child again, joyfully naked. The bears held paws and danced around me in a circle. We sang together. They protected and adored me. Then—as I knew would happen, the foreknowledge lending betrayal to their song—they began to leer and sneer. Their eyes shone with malice. They closed in about me. I was naked, and their teeth gleamed sharp and white against the sepia.

I ran from them, ducking under their interlocked paws, pricking my skin on hairs as sharp as the pen that had drawn them. I ran and ran and ran to the edge of a precipice and awakened just as they were about to catch me.

The first time I dreamt this dream at St. Paul's, I expected to wake up on Addison Street in West Philadelphia. But there were no city noises to comfort me, and no headlights sweeping like searchlights across the blinds.

I dreamt that I was watching my own funeral. I was a small, grayish corpse in a short coffin. From the back of the church I could see the tips of my feet and my folded hands above the polished mahogany. I observed the mourning with self-absorbed satisfaction.

In another dream, I was walking on the sidewalk on Addison Street toward my friend Siboney to ask if she wanted to play. Under my feet the sidewalk shimmered with broken glass. Then the shimmering became movement. The cement squares began to shift. They had been shifting, in fact, from the beginning of time. The solidity had been an illusion. So, too, had been the unbroken surface. Holes yawned between the squares, small ones, then bigger and bigger. They emitted radiant heat and the sounds of souls in despair. An anthropomorphic sea of magma howled and gurgled fire. I had to walk. I had to walk the walk, but at every step, the holes swirled around. If I made one wrong step, I would tumble into hell.

I did not talk about my nightmare vision in religion class, but I thought about it. I did not speak to the girls in my room about the bears, but I thought of them, too, while I laughed and listened for betrayal. The bears warned me to beware of slipping into friendship.

Girls came and went in my room. I liked it that way. I wanted the company—and the prosperous appearance of company. They taught me about tollhouse cookies; Switzerland; the names of automobiles, shampoos, rock groups, Connecticut cities; casual shoes and outdoor-equipment catalogues. I learned that other girls, too, tired during sports, that their calf muscles, like mine, screamed out pain when they walked down the stairs. I learned about brands of tampons. I learned that these girls thought their hair dirty when they did not wash it daily.

"I hear what you're saying, but I just don't see it. I'm looking at your hair, but I don't see grease."

"Oh, my God, it's, like, hanging down in clumps!" One girl

pulled a few strands from her scalp to display the offending sheen. "Look."

I learned that their romanticized lusts sounded like mine felt, as did their ambivalent homesickness, and their guarded, girlish competitiveness.

As they came to sit and stay, however, differences emerged between us. Taken together, these girls seemed more certain than I that they deserved our good fortune. They were sorry for people who were poorer than they, but they did not feel guilty to think of the resources we were sucking up—forests, meadows and ponds, the erudition of well-educated teachers, water for roaring showers, heat that blew out of opened windows everywhere, food not eaten but mixed together for disgusting fun after lunch. They took it as their due. It was boot-camp preparation for America's leaders, which we were told we would one day be. They gave no indication that they worried that others, smarter or more worthy, might, at that very moment, be giving up hope of getting what we had.

I did not, however, tell the girls what I was thinking. We did not talk about how differently we saw the world. Indeed my black and their white heritage was not a starting point for our relationship, but rather was the outer boundary. I could not cross it, because there sprang up a hard wall of denial impervious to my inexperienced and insecure assault. "Well, as far as I'm concerned," one girl after another would say, "it doesn't matter to me if somebody's white or black or green or purple. I mean people are just people."

The motion, having been made, would invariably be seconded.

"Really. I mean, it's the person that counts."

Having castigated whites' widespread inability to see individuals for the skin in which they were wrapped, I could hardly argue with "it's the person that counts." I didn't know why they always chose green and purple to dramatize their indifference, but my ethnicity seemed diminished when the talk turned to Muppets. It was like they were taking something from me.

"I'm not purple." What else could you say?

"The truth is," somebody said, "I . . . this is *so* silly . . . I'm really embarrassed, but, it's like, there *are* some things you, God, you just feel ashamed to admit that you think about this stuff, but I always kind of wondered if, like, black guys and white guys were, like, different . . ."

They shrieked with laughter. Sitting on the afghan my mother had crocheted for me in the school colors of red and white, their rusty-dusty feet all over my good afghan, they laughed and had themselves a ball.

"Now, see, that's why people don't want to say anything," one girl said. "Look, you're getting all mad."

"I'm not mad."

"You look it."

"I'm not mad. I don't even know about any differences between white guys and black guys," I said deliberately avoiding the word boys. (Black manhood seemed at stake. Everything seemed at stake.) Then I added as archly as possible: "I don't mess around with white boys."

The party broke up soon after. I sat still, the better to control my righteous anger. It always came down to this, I thought, the old song of the South. I wanted something more meaningful. I wanted it to mean something that I had come four hundred miles from home, and sat day after day with them in Chapel, in class. I wanted it to mean something that after Martin Luther King's and Malcolm X's assassinations, we kids sweated together in sports, ate together at Seated Meal, studied and talked together at night. It couldn't be just that I was to become like them or hang onto what I'd been. It couldn't be that lonely and pointless.

I looked across the quad to Jimmy's window, and waved. He

was not in his room, but the mere sight of his lighted window brought me back to my purpose. It was not to run my ass ragged trying to wrench some honesty out of this most disingenuous of God's people. I had come to St. Paul's to turn it out. How had I lost sight of the simple fact?

In a few days "inside" grades for the Fall Term caught me by surprise. I had barely settled in. During reports the Rector said that interim grades were merely to give us an idea of our progress. Students called them "warning" grades. Groupmasters handed them to each student in the evening.

I churned with anticipation all day. At one moment it seemed to me that I'd been doing brilliantly. I was understanding Sr. Fuster's musical Spanish, speaking glibly in religion about "systems of belief," hiding from Mr. Buxton the crush I was developing, trooping good-naturedly through the inanity of trigonometry, drawing and redrawing the folds of a draped cloth in art.

One wrong answer, however, would change my perspective completely. Sure, I was understanding Sr. Fuster better, but my essays were grammatical disasters. In religion, I skittered over the surface of the language, never quite knowing what I meant to say until the moment I opened my mouth. I only *thought* Mr. Buxton hadn't noticed my crush. I had fallen asleep during eighth-period trig. In art class, my colors were timid; my perspective was off.

Mr. Hawley handed me the thin piece of paper on which the computer in the Schoolhouse basement had recorded my warning grades. On my sheet were five grades, two Honors and three High Passes. What I saw when I looked at my warning grades were two Bs and three Cs. The school had made it quite clear in the catalog and elsewhere that St. Paul's grades were not letter-grade equivalents. They'd told us that High Honors were rare as A-pluses, and that Honors meant just that. No matter. I saw average. I saw failure. And what I saw on that paper, Mr. Hawley saw in my face.

"There are several things about these warning grades you should keep in mind," he said. "The first is that although they may look like real grades and feel like real grades, they are not real grades.

"OK. Now, how accurate an indicator are these? Well, I'm sure that in some of your courses, there hasn't been enough work assigned and graded for teachers to evaluate. And in that case, many teachers feel safer grading on the low side, just so that no one gets a false sense of security. So, it is possible that you might be doing better than these grades, and it is extremely unlikely that you'd be doing any worse."

He told me that High Passes were not the end of the world. "The other thing that I doubt you are giving yourself credit for," he said, "is that you've just come in, as a new Fifth Former—not many people come in the Fifth Form, as you've noticed, and there's a reason why, many reasons—and you've just come straight from your old hometown high. Some of these other students have had a different preparation. I am certain that you'll catch on fast. Look, you *have* caught on fast. I've got old girls in this house who'd kill for those grades. But the fact is, I don't see how you can expect much more of yourself right now."

Mr. Hawley told me that he'd seen students take a year or two to adjust to St. Paul's, not just public-school students, but kids from fancy day schools.

"I've only *got* two years," I said.

"You're doing great."

When girls on my hall asked about my grades, I joked: "It's like when the Ghost of Christmas Yet To Come points to the gravestone," I said. "All I want to know is: Is this what will be or what may be?"

"Oh, you'll do fine."

I wondered if anyone here had ever expected me to do better than this. White faces of the adults flashed in my head, smiling, encouraging, tilted to one side, asking if I'd like to talk, extending their welcome. "If you need anything . . ." Early on they'd told me that I'd do fine. I felt betrayed, first by them, then by my own naiveté. HPs were probably what they'd meant by fine—for black scholarship kids. Maybe that's what they'd been saying all along, only I hadn't heard it.

No sooner had the furor of warning grades subsided than the excitement of Parents' Day began. A few parents appeared on the last Friday afternoon in October, and by Saturday morning they were everywhere, cars clogging the roads, adult voices filling the Schoolhouse, where they waited in long lines for ten-minute talks with our teachers.

Parents who had no money or no time did not come, but mine did. And so did my grandparents. They surrounded me as we walked slowly along the paths. Seeing them made me know how much I'd missed them. I guided them through the days' activities as if marching through a dream.

In the evening, they came to the show we'd prepared for them. I sang in the chorus, and they saw me sing. I showed them my books and my papers. I walked them to each of my favorite places along the paths and pointed out where gardeners had been working all week to spruce up the grounds. My father remembered that dorm proctors at Lincoln University had handed out fresh new blankets on anniversary weekends, just before festivities, and then collected them again when parents went home. We laughed about that. But St. Paul's was no Lincoln, they kept saying, that tiny black college in rural Pennsylvania where milk from the nearby cows had tasted of onion grass in the spring.

I recalled the photographs of my father and his classmates, young black men with shiny hair, baring their legs and hamming it up for the camera; the photo of my father and mother, who had married the Saturday before my father graduated. They stood under a huge old tree, grinning broadly, my mother in her pedal-pusher pants, her body curving like an S against his, her arm waving in the air. Every time one of us mentioned Lincoln—and we did, again and again, because it was the only college we knew well—I thought of those photographs. As often as I saw the image in my mind, I heard snatches of what had been their old favorite song:

> . . . Our day will come
> And we'll have ev'rything,
> We'll share the joy
> Falling in love can bring.
> No one can tell me that I'm too young to know
> I love you so,
> And you love me . . .
> Our day wi-ill come.

I could not stop thinking of them like that, their arms entwined like the branches of a mulberry, certain that they would do together what their parents had been unable to do. "We decided we were *not* going to end up divorced. We just decided it," they always said. I'd wondered how they could have been so sure. "Our dreams have magic because we'll always stay/In love this way/Our day will come."

Lincoln looked green in the pictures, and, as if it were not full enough with their promise, and the promise of so many young men, black Greeks, black gods ready to march out into the world and grab it for their own, it was also home to the prepubescent Julian Bond "just running around the campus like any other little faculty kid," and, he, of course, was now in government.

My mother lit a cigarette in my room, and my father made a face. I could not take my eyes off the pack. My mother had changed brands. So absorbed had I been with my own changes, that I had not expected any from them, and my mother least of all. It was a small thing, the brand of cigarettes, but it occurred to me for the first time that in leaving home, I gave up the right to know the details of their daily life. Things might be the same when I got back for the next vacation, or they might not. I had no way of knowing, because I wasn't there.

Whatever I had planned to tell them—about how I did not feel like myself here, how I was worried that the recruiters expected little more than survival from us, how I was beginning to doubt that they could *see* excellence in us, because it might pop out through thick lips and eyes or walk on flat feet or sit on big, bodacious behinds—I kept to myself. I showed off my familiarity with my new school. Why, I was fitting in fine. My teachers said so. My new friends said so—Hey, girls, come meet my folks. . . .

Soon they had to leave. Because it was more convenient, St. Paul's School did not switch to Standard Time until Sunday night when the parents were gone. My family was amused by the custom; I was not. "It's just like St. Paul's. It's practically a metaphor," I said ("metaphor" having become one of my favorite new words), "for the arrogance of this place. Isn't that the most arrogant thing you've ever seen, just changing *time!*"

"Well, honey," said my grandmother, "it's just for a little while. It's not as if they were going to keep it that way."

"When you think about it, it's an arbitrary change anyway," my father said. "And now that we need to save energy, who knows whether they might just change it some more to take better advantage of the daylight."

Everyone smiled mildly at me as if I were being unreasonable. I let the subject drop.

I fell asleep that night listening to the country sounds that replaced the parents' festive noise. In the branches, dead limbs creaked like old doors. Every hour until midnight the Chapel tower's metallic throat pealed out the wrong time, sharp and bright and sure.

November set in cold and damp. The work of the school chugged along: *I think I can, I think I can, I think I can.* The chipper refrain from childhood came chugging through my mind as I ran through the rain between classes. I did not have a raincoat that fall. *I think I can I think I can I think I can.* I slogged around the muddy field and hurled myself through wind sprints. Browner mud, grayer skies, blacker water. The wind penetrated the fiber of my clothing. The sun did not. But the engine of the school chugged on. Work and more work, with no way to get out. People and more people, with no way to get away from them, the same people day after day, becoming more familiar, their walks, their accents, their quirks and behavior. They said the same things, cracked the same jokes. So did I. I bored myself. We bored each other. Our teasing grew less witty and meaner.

It was in November that my soccer team played one of the boys' club teams. Our coach urged us to play aggressively. The ball flew up and down the field. I cursed its every reversal, knowing that I'd have to turn around and run back down the same field I'd just run up. Back and forth and back and forth, meaninglessly, mercilessly. The ball zinged, and I ran parallel to it, out on the edge of the field, in wing position, just like I didn't have any better sense. The drudgery was punctuated now and then by panic when a ball popped toward me. "Close up the hole! Close up the hole! Take it down. You're free, you're free!" and then I'd see the expanse of field between me and the goal, and I'd know that I could not tag along, but would have to run fast, faster than the mob coming at me. I wheezed and ran and wheezed. I opened my mouth wide, but I felt as if I were sucking air through a straw.

I think I can I think I can I think I can. Up jumped the good little girl inside, ever hopeful, she who believed that all she needed was one more win. Up she jumped as if this were a fifth-grade penmanship contest, the tie-breaker in a spelling bee, an audition for *Annie Get Your Gun:* "Anything you can do I can do better, I can do anything better than you." I knew this little girl. She looked like the freckled six-year-old in my mother's wallet. She felt like Pollyanna.

The ball came at me. The crazy little girl inside tore after it. Girls who had beaten me in wind sprints were unable to catch me. My arms pumped up and down as I ran. They helped push me forward. Maybe this was it, I thought, maybe. I almost cried with gratitude. Asthma came to clamp round my chest, but this time I was not afraid of suffocating. I huffed puffs of steam into the cold air.

I didn't see the little guy who came to steal the ball. I didn't see him at all until he was right in front of me like a sudden insult. I was stunned. The ball was mine. The goal was in sight. I could see the goal tender's fear, his awkward alarm. I loved how he called out to his fullbacks—as if they could stop me. But who was this little guy who would not be moved?

He put out his foot to snag the ball. He got it, and pulled it just to the side of me. I scooped the ball back with the inside of my foot, and knew I had to move it again, but could not, because he was there, the little guy again, his cleat coming, slender and tenacious. Then I charged. There was screaming around us, coming closer. I had to have the ball. I had to drive it in. I didn't realize I had fallen until the impact of the hard ground went up through my hip and reverberated inside my head. The ball rolled away. The whistle blew, and they stopped the game for us. His face contorted to hold back his tears. Clouds drifted overhead, wispy and beautiful.

I saw him a couple days later. He swung himself gingerly between his crutches as if his armpits were sore. He smiled bravely at me.

"I'm sorry," I said to him, trying to feel more intensely the throbbing in the purplish lump that had appeared on the side of my own leg.

"That's all right," he said, shrugging his shoulders above the crutches. "You couldn't help it. Are you all right?"

"Sure. Got a bruise or two." I felt like a brutish distortion of those big, black women I so admired, like Sojourner Truth as the actresses portrayed her: "Ah kin push a plow as far as a man—*And ain't I a voman?!*"

I worked harder the rest of the term than I had ever known I could work. I looked up more vocabulary words and wrote papers and practiced grammar. I worked and reworked trigonometry equations. I took to paraphrasing an old nun I'd once seen in a movie. She croaks at the girl whom the Virgin Mary has visited: "I have read the words of our Lord God until my eyes burned like the very fires of hell. Why should God choose *you?*"

No longer convinced of the special brilliance I had once expected to discover in myself, no longer certain that my blackness gave me precocious wisdom, or that I could outslick these folks, I held onto that crazy old nun. They might be smarter than I or better prepared or more athletic. They might know the rules better, whatever the unspoken rules were for leaping to the top of this world and staying there. But I could work. I could read until my eyes burned like the very fires of hell! I could outwork them all. (Ain't I a voman?) Will, it seemed to me, was the only quality I had in greater abundance than my fellows, and I would will myself to work.

Examinations were the test of my resolve. During exams there were no more classes and no more sports, only studying, and for big stakes—exams were worth large fractions of our final grades. I felt the rush of pure competition. Studying distracted me from other people, thoughts, worries.

At the appointed hour we walked to the gymnasium, where folding tables and chairs were arranged in rows on white mats that muffled the noise of our footsteps. Blue books were stacked, fresh and clean, on the front desks. Teachers handed out their questions and smiled encouragement. Our religion exam asked one question in its final section: "Who is Jesus?"

I was unprepared for the question—and for the gusher of feelings it released. Suddenly it mattered to me that in His name the red-bearded men, missionaries, soldiers, capitalists, adventurists all, clambered over the earth as if it were a woman's body; that in Jesus' name they triumphed and we suffered, and in Jesus' name, too—for Christ's sake—we both claimed justice, oh, and looked for the faith to unite:

> Join hands, then, brothers of the faith
> Whate'er your race may be!
> Who serves my Father as a son
> Is surely kin to me.

(We sang it in chapel, John Oxenham's words—he had a name—set to the generic "Negro melody" in the hymnal.)

It mattered to me to get it right about Him: the lamb-shepherd-bridegroom-buffoon, the Way and the Light, the dreamy boy on the calendars tacked onto the wall over my great-grandmother's side of the bed. It mattered, though I could not write it, and there was no place for it, that she criticized and judged, that she told us, with reference to the color of the man we should marry: Don't darken your bread. It mattered that when she died she took with her any hope of her approval, so long withheld, but so close that at times we nearly had it. She'd snatched it back into the grave with her like a setting sun pulling the last streaks of light from the sky.

The blue-eyed boy over the bed, talking to the elders at the temple, holding His hands out to the children: Only He would love those unworthy of love. He was the bridegroom, the resurrection, and the light. I wanted so to believe, to make what Tillich called "the leap of faith." I imagined myself jumping at a brick wall, naked, bruised, leaping at a garden beyond. My head filled with noise and pictures, scraps of music from Hollywood Bible epics, the remembered tastes of the papery African Methodist Episcopal wafer and grape juice, and the comfort of sucking my own fleshy thumb at night. *Take, eat.* God only knows what I actually wrote.

By the time the exams were collected, I arose, stiff and tremulous. I had no idea how I would face studying for the next, or sitting to write it, letting loose in my head so much noise and chaos in the quiet, orderly gym.

But I did. We all did, again and again until it was over.

Just three months after my parents had delivered me to St. Paul's I was on my way home again. Fumiko came with me. On the bus to the station, I buzzed with exhaustion and anticipation. One student in the back of the bus pulled out a joint; a couple of others passed bottles in brown paper bags.

"Have some?"

As we drove through the Merrimack River valley, I thought of the winos' street-corner toast:

> *If wine was a river and I was a duck*
> *I'd dive to the bottom and never come up,*
> *But since wine ain't no river, and I ain't no duck,*
> *I'ma drink this wine 'til I'm fucked up.*

"No, thanks," I said. I used an off-handed voice and lit a cigarette to show my cool. My mother would have killed me had I arrived with liquor on my breath. I could smell it even as Fumiko and I dozed.

I thought and then dreamt about the wet necks of bottles everywhere, and about a glamorous adulthood, when I would drink, not out of a bottle, but from thin glasses clinking ice cubes. I loved ice. I thought about a girl at school who made piña coladas, and in a blender, no less, before Seated Meal— the very drink my grandmother and her friends sipped ("Oh, no, my dear, just one for me; these things sneak up on you!") at their club dinners. I thought about my other grandmother, who drank until cheap Scotch released the rage within her and the insatiable hunger: for more life, more beauty, more men, more food, more love, more money, more luck. I thought of her asleep on the toilet and awake the next morning, the smell of Scotch excreting from the fine pores of her velvety skin, of her toothless shame and the guilty, secretive search for her teeth. I thought of her soprano voice, that was cracked and pitted now by alcohol and tobacco. How could you have a voice like that and destroy it? I wondered. How could you live with yourself?

When I could bear my own homecoming thoughts no longer, I turned to Fumiko. We made excited eyes and talk together. She was an excellent traveling companion and, when we arrived home, a perfect houseguest. Fumiko's exquisite Japanese manners delighted my family. She brought gifts: pink-and-white-faced dolls with embroidered kimonos and silky black hair. My mother installed them in the china closet where they still reign. After a trans-Pacific phone call, her parents shipped us a five-gallon keg of Japan's best soy sauce.

Whenever my family seemed in danger of confusing Fumiko and her dolls, I warned them pedantically: they were not to make geisha-girl cracks; they were not to treat her as if she did not speak English; they were not to pull out their five facts about Japan for her confirmation and agreement.

In fact, my mother recognized without any help from me that Fumiko was a teenager, mischievous, full of hormones, and in need of maternal guidance. When Fumiko announced that she had given our telephone number to a Philly-born boy she'd met at another prep school, my mother set strict visitation rules.

"If that child thinks that I'm letting her waltz out of this house with some Puerto Rican from North Philly, she'd better think again."

"Oh, Mom, he's not 'some Puerto Rican,' " I said archly. (More and more often, I found myself mortified by my family's lack of Third World unity.) "He's a guy who goes to a prep school . . . just like we do."

"*I* don't know him. I promised that girl's parents that I would be a mother to her just like I'm a mother to my own children. I tell you what: I would not want anyone to let my child go off in some strange city with some strange man they'd never even met. That is *not* my idea of looking out for a young girl, and despite what you all may think about yourselves and your independence, the fact is that you *are* still children, and I *am* still mother.

"And besides," she continued, taking another tack, no doubt because of some scrap of resistance in my face, "let me tell you one thing. Some of the weirdest people I know are educated people. Why? I don't know. But the fact that he's a preppie doesn't mean a damn thing to me. I am not impressed by education. He could be even crazier than he would have been had he stayed home in North Philly!"

So Fumiko's admirer came to visit on a weekday afternoon (not evening). The trip took an hour and a half on public transportation. ("I am *not* using up my gas and my day to

chauffeur some boy. If he can't find his way, with that education he's getting, well, shame on him.") When he arrived, my
mother made a face to indicate that he was bigger than she'd
expected. He had a bigger bush, and a hat that he made the
mistake of leaving on in our house. Something else was wrong,
too.

My mother and I went into the kitchen to leave them alone
together. We closed the door. "I'm sorry," my mother said
after a minute. "I can't take this any longer."

"Oh, Mama, please," I whispered. "It's just for a little while.
My Lord, you've only given them an hour or two. How much
could a little funk hurt in one hour?"

"A little funk? Is that what they're teaching you? You don't
smell like that. Not yet at least. God knows that child doesn't
smell at all."

"Japanese don't smell."

"That's the goofiest thing you've said yet. I know *he* smells,
though, and I can't have it. I just cannot have it."

"What are you going to do?"

My mother looked at me scornfully and mounted the staircase. I was aware that I was placing the tender feelings of this
big, funky dude ahead of my mother's sovereignty in her own
house. I spent a few idle moments wishing that they had gone
to the movies as they'd wanted. I had promised to chaperone.
Then I spent a few more moments cursing my mother's need
to lord it over us that this was her house. Her house. I had
thought St. Paul's would have freed me of all that, but instead,
I was back here getting double doses, just so I wouldn't forget
under the subversive tutelage of those people, people who obviously had no control over their own children. Mom had several complaints about what those people were doing to me:
they had me eating too fast, dumping pepper on my food as if
she hadn't already seasoned it just right, neglecting to wash my
hands frequently enough, forgetting to mind my tongue. By the

time I had done thinking and sighing, my mother returned from upstairs.

She stood on the landing. "Now I want to do a little something," she announced to the pair on the brown brocade couch, worn shiny in patches.

"What is it?" Fumiko asked, prettily biting her consonants.

"Close your eyes, everybody!" Mama's voice was falsely bright.

I knew that tone. I watched her with suspicious dread from the kitchen. Then I saw them close their eyes, and my mother pulled from behind her back an aerosol can of deodorant.

"Keep them closed!" she sang.

She sprayed all around them, making sure to get some mist on the big, odoriferous interloper. Then she opened the window behind them a crack to let in the winter air.

"Just a funny little family custom," she said to Fumiko as she floated back into the kitchen. "There," she said to me. "All done! Just like a needle at the doctor's."

I visited Karen and Ruthie. They asked how St. Paul's was, and whether or not I liked it. I wanted to answer them honestly. I wanted them to know how my life had changed so that we could sit down in the dim light of Karen's living room and talk about it. But I did not have enough words or time to make them see it and feel it with me, and besides, nobody, not even my best friends, cared as much about St. Paul's as its students. Nobody else lived there. They lived, as we Paulies joked, in the real world.

Fumiko told them in her halting English that St. Paul's was "very hard." I agreed, and once they laughed, I broke into the monologue that I repeated, with variations according to the audience, for years: "First of all, you've got to understand that the teachers are all a little screwy. You've got to be to stay in a place like that for twenty years. These are the people who decided to opt out of real life at some point, and they are set loose on us twenty-four hours a day.

"OK? You got the picture? There is no escape from these people. They are out to *improve* you: how you read, how you write, how you run, how you look, what you say at the dinner table, how you *think*. You see what I mean by no escape? Meanwhile, back at the dorm, the white kids are blasting the hardest hard rock you've ever heard. . . ."

Later, I figured, when I understood the school better, then I could talk to them seriously about it. For now, I wanted to make them laugh. I wanted to entertain. I didn't dare risk being boring or snobbish or cry-babyish about my new school. I didn't want to lose them.

"Now you tell me about everybody at Yeadon. How was the new majorette squad this season? Did Mr. Cenatempo let you do flaming batons this year?"

Each time we began a new subject, I needed them to fill me in on facts, and I had to fill Fumiko in. I didn't know what they'd just read in English, or who had sung the solos in this year's *Messiah,* or what prank Bob Bailey had pulled in science lab. Too much exposition weighed down our conversation. We couldn't anticipate each other anymore or jump back and forth between subjects until we landed in intimate territory. I was with my friends, but I could not get the full pleasure of them. I wanted to weep with frustration.

Two nights before we returned to school, I stayed up by myself drinking my mother's Christmas liqueur late into the night. I decided to level with myself. My new friends and I knew each other's daily routines, but we had no history—and no future, I thought, when we all went back to our real lives. But back in real life, Karen and Ruthie and I, once past the memories, had to work hard just to keep talking. At my own house I felt as if I were fighting for a new position in the family

order, while Mama pretended not to notice and Dad maybe
didn't notice for real. Everywhere I went I felt out of place.
The fact was that I had left home in September gleeful and
smug. I took it as divine justice that now I felt as if I no longer
belonged anywhere.

Chapter Six

I returned to St. Paul's that winter with a definite agenda. I would earn at least straight Honors. I would get myself elected to the Student Council if I had to make nice with every girl in my house. I decided to take biology, and despite my fears, I signed up for calculus, too. Mr. Hawley advised against six courses, but in the end, I had my way. Once I was settled—back in the groove with Jimmy, used to my new classes, elected as Simpson's Council representative—I felt ready to make public my fledgling romance.

Ricky Lockhart had been more pen pal than boyfriend until then. We'd met at a party in the fall, and had since corresponded. When his brightly colored envelopes appeared in my mailbox, my girlfriends and I made a fuss on the way to lunch. Not only were his letters flattering, they were convenient: I had an excuse for not spending my boarding-school career hanging onto the elbow of some boy at St. Paul's (which was what going steady seemed to mean for a girl). Ricky wrote that he adored me; he pined for me. All that and freedom, too. The boys in the Third World took to saying that I'd made him up and was mailing letters to myself.

Meanwhile, Ricky and I were making plans for him to visit me at school. He would bear scrutiny. Ricky was as beautiful as an African sculpture, with skin as smooth as roasted coffee beans, high cheekbones, and nostrils that flared when he laughed. At his prep school, he played varsity football, raced on the bicycling team, and played basketball in the winter. He loved computer programming. And he was a senior. The oldest of three children from Schenectady, New York, he, too, was on a mission. He addressed my letters in perfect, black calligraphy, and asked me to perfume my letters to him.

Maldonado agreed to let Ricky stay in his room, and Ricky and I exchanged a flurry of short, practical letters to set the date. He would arrive after classes on a Saturday afternoon, and stay until early Sunday evening.

Not only romance, but new friendships were sprouting. I spent more time in the evenings with Annette, the Third Former from Chicago whom I'd met that first afternoon in Simpson's lobby. Through her I met Grace, a Chinese-American who had gravitated to the Third World group. She came to the meetings, first with Annette, and then by herself. She sat at our lunch table and became one of us. Grace and I petitioned for permission to room together by converting my room into a bedroom and hers, down the hall, into a study. The housemasters conferred. For a hundred years and more, we were told, the school's policy had been to allow boys to room only with their formmates, but since girls matured faster and in less predictable patterns, they would let us have a go at our novel idea. Miss Deane, Grace's groupmaster, cautioned me to remember, however, that as a Fifth Former, I probably had more influence than I knew on my Third Form roommate, and that I needed to behave accordingly. Great, I thought guiltily. I've already encouraged her to smoke, but I was determined to do better in the future. A couple of weeks before Ricky was due to visit, Grace and I made our move.

I could hardly believe how organized she was: removing her contacts, putting on her glasses, brushing her hair fifty strokes, then face and teeth—on it went each night, a precise ritual, perfectly efficient and never missed, as consistent as an adult.

She seemed amused that I belonged to the Astronomy Club, an activity I could not dodge in the cold midwinter, because Mr. Hawley was its adviser. He banged on my door as he hustled past on subzero nights when the New Hampshire air stretched cloudless and clear to the ends of the universe. A handful of us met at the old observatory at the end of the fields. The others were the school science buffs, white boys, pimply, young. We made corny science jokes together. Away from my cooler friends, I giggled happily.

Through the cold lens stars appeared as close as shaved glass in a kaleidoscope. The moon took on a vague landscape, pitted and creased.

Throughout the winter I looked for the constellations: I pointed them out to my friends—Orion, the passionate hunter, and the seven sisters, called Pleiades, whom he chased—eager to show off my knowledge, and yet reluctant to reveal how affected I was by my new relation to the heavens. One of the Pleiades hid because of her shame. I looked for her as if she were a friend. The sky hung as close to me that winter as it had in my childhood, when it covered the dark alleys behind our Philadelphia row houses like a dropped ceiling from God. Out in the night with the sky stretched taut overhead, I could feel it again, my right place in the universe: infinitely small, but nearly tall enough to touch the sky.

It was on such a Friday night that I stood by the post-office telephone waiting for Ricky to ring. We had arranged that he'd call to confirm his arrival the next day. I was watching the lights of the library shimmering across the pond, and planning to take Ricky to the observatory the next night, when the phone rang.

"Is that you?" His voice sounded delicious and near.

I laughed to hear him. "Yes. It's me."

"Guess where I am."

"You're not at school?"

"I'm in town."

"You're in town this late?"

"No, silly. Your town, Concord, New Hampshire."

"You are?"

"I found a way to get out of my commitment for tomorrow morning. And I couldn't bear to wait all day to see you."

He was two miles away. What was I going to do with him? I had filled out the card requesting permission for a weekend guest to stay in Maldonado's room, but the permission was for Saturday night only. Any changes had to be filed with the Vice-Rector's office by the Wednesday before the weekend. I couldn't ask Maldonado to hide him for the night, and I couldn't tell him to go back.

"Aren't you glad?"

"Sure. I'm just trying to think how to smuggle you in."

"I hope this won't cause any trouble for you. I should have called before."

"No, this is great! Just let me think." I told him to catch a taxi and have it drop him off at the entrance to the school. I'd wait for him there.

I rushed to Simpson. Grace would be in our room changing from her dinner clothes into pants.

"Thank God you're back," I said. "Listen. Ricky's here."

"I thought he was coming tomorrow."

"He was, but he's here now."

She laughed. "Uh-oh. I guess that's my cue."

"Where else can I put him?"

"The guys wouldn't mind hiding him."

"But then they could get in trouble."

"Not as much trouble as you could if you're thinking what I think you're thinking."

"Oh, God. Oh, God." I wailed. Ruthie Belding appeared at the door. She lived across the hall.

"What's wrong?"

I looked at Ruthie hard and tried to judge whether or not I could trust her. All I could see as I looked at her, however, were her snow boots. She always had the appropriate footwear, I thought, conscious of my wet feet. Ruthie tossed her cornsilk hair. The other girls never tired of saying how beautiful she was. She and I worked together on the balance beam.

"Well, come on. There's a mighty big secret here, and I'm dying to know."

"Listen, Ruthie. My friend is here. He's here. He'll be here, at school, in minutes."

"Ooooh, Libby." The nickname Pam Hudson gave me had stuck. I wasn't crazy about it, but I got used to it. "You naughty girl."

"Oh, Ruthie, please. I've got to get him in. It's all cleared for him to stay over at Conover House tomorrow night, but he just showed up early."

"Just showed up? Libby!"

"I'll clear out," Grace said.

"You could spend the night with me," Ruthie volunteered.

Grace looked at me and laughed. "Don't look like that. Your face'll give you away."

"Right," I said. "Listen, I've got to go get him. Could you *please* stick around to help me sneak him in?"

I met Ricky walking along the road into campus. In the dark I studied his features again, and was relieved to see that he was as good-looking as I'd remembered. He was also as ardent as his letters.

"We can't kiss out here," I whispered.

He laughed his low, quiet laugh. I began to hope that we might pull it off after all.

Grace met us at the back door. I left her with Ricky while I ran upstairs to check the hallway, then signaled them to go up. Once the three of us were in the room, we sighed together and then burst out laughing, Ricky with his hand over his mouth.

I do not remember much until after check-in, when the flushing and tooth-brushing and door-swinging subsided and the hallway grew quiet. I do remember that I went into the bathroom to get undressed and into my longest, thickest flannel nightgown, and that I brushed my teeth until my gums were sore.

I remember insisting, after our excited talk together, that I had to finish my calculus homework for Saturday-morning class. No doubt I could have used Ricky's help. I don't think I asked.

Later we had a long discussion about sleeping arrangements. We tried to keep it light-hearted, like a '30s comedy. I began the night, swaddled in my flannel nightgown, in Grace's bed. Her pillowcase smelled dry like her hair. Ricky and I talked across the room. He wanted me to come to my bed, and I told him no, as I'd always said before.

I'd said it to Washington, even though I had not wanted to say it to *him*. I'd said it to Russell on the night of Yeadon's prom when he drove up a road I'd never seen, parked in the mist, and told me only half-jokingly that I'd never find my way home. But I had not wanted Russell, so it had been easy to bust out of his car like a SWAT team, and walk into the drizzle in my turquoise-and-white gown and *peau de soie* shoes until he relented and drove me, unmolested, to the after-party we had planned to attend.

I'd said no before, but before, I'd had only to get back to my front door to make it stick, and then the big stone-and-stucco house took me in to where the judo black-belt father slept. (Boys joked about being afraid of him, which was how I learned that they were.) Before, we'd had only to subdue ourselves for a few hours. In my old world, everybody but the most in love or the most careless did the same. I was supported by the knowledge that my girlfriends were out on dates, in cars, on porches, in living rooms, with or without parents nearby, fighting the same fight. We'd all kiss goodnight at the same time in different doorways, with the same longing, tragic and moist.

Here there was no doorway. I could hear him breathing, and when he lay down his voice curled around deep in his chest. The room was full of him. My stone house, my black-belt father, my ubiquitous mother, my intrusive little sister, and yappy dog were four hundred miles away. I talked and talked, desperate to make time pass, until I had nothing left to talk about.

We said no more, but my room was not quiet. The air buzzed with a hormonal hum like a burglar alarm. I closed my eyes tight.

"Listen, it's silly for you to sleep over there. I know you don't want to do anything. But does that mean we can't hold each other? Just hug?"

I got up and went to my bed. He turned on his side to make room. I liked the feeling of curling up next to him, and resting my head on his arm.

"Is my head too heavy?"

"Are you kidding?"

I did fall asleep, and just the way I always did. ("It's weird," Pam Hudson said. "You really do just 'drop off.' People always say that they drop off, but you really do it.")

I dropped off in his arms, and I began to dream. Then in my dream I heard somebody shushing me. I had to get out of where I was. I had to shout, but someone shushed me. I opened my eyes and saw his form, just his form, above me. I only saw him from the shoulders up. I heard him saying my name again and again and again, and I felt a sharp pain, small and piercing, somewhere I could not at first locate. Then it was a big, blunt pain, dull and stupid like a bowel movement in the wrong place.

"I couldn't help it," he said. "You were so beautiful there on my arm."

Then I knew what was happening, and I strained to see his face. This facelessness was too awful with the pushing and pushing in the dark. Suddenly, I didn't like his smell. I searched in my mind for a word, as if a word would save me from this stupidity, the dull, dark, stupid feeling. *If you flag my train* . . . I wouldn't have those words. I wanted other words. *Might as well take a ride.* . . . I didn't want it like this. I didn't want it. I hated myself.

I began to cry just as he finished, and he misconstrued my sobs at first. He kissed me delightedly and told me he loved me, and then he felt my tears and pulled his face back to see. Now that it was over I could see his features again. I could see the light from the moon on the tight skin and sculpted mouth. I could see his eyes, searching and searching my face. "Was this your first time?"

I wanted to scream.

"*Your first time?* I didn't know. I didn't know," he said.

I tried to believe him, but I could not stop crying.

Then he cried, too. "I'm so sorry," he said. "I didn't mean to hurt you. I never want to hurt you. I just couldn't help it. God, I'm so sorry."

We comforted each other in the awkward way of adolescents, each of us absorbed in ourselves, unable to console the other, until I jumped up in bed. Pregnant! I could be pregnant, I thought. I leapt out of the bed.

"I've got to go to the bathroom," I said. The bright white lights in the hallway nearly blinded me, and they were brighter still in the bathroom. I threw off my nightgown and stepped into the shower, trying to remember scraps of the women's conversation. Why hadn't I listened more carefully? Aunt Evie had once said something about a woman whom she knew who had been too dumb to use birth control. "The least she could have done," Aunt Evie had said, "was wash some of that out and give herself a fighting chance. The fewer of those little tadpoles swimming around, the better."

I washed as if to rid myself of sin and shame, and, ignoring the scum in the tub, I lay down under the spigot and did the best I knew how. Earlier in the year, I had coached a girlfriend from a strict Catholic family to insert a tampon.

"Joanne," I'd shouted over the stall, "you've got to feel for the hole."

"No! Do I have to?"

"Yes. You've got three openings. . . ."

"Three?"

"Yes!"

"Where's the third one?"

"That depends on which two you've already found."

Lying under the punishing spigot, I asked God to forgive me for having laughed at her. God knows, I thought to myself, I'm just as ignorant, and worse. Joanne hadn't been dumb enough to get herself knocked up.

In the mirror I looked, as my mother would have said, like the wild woman of Borneo. I dared not think what else she would have said. My hair had shot up on the back of my head like turkey tail feathers, and my eyes were swollen and red. Sex goddess! I taunted myself and then replaced my flannel nightgown as if to shield me from further damage.

We went to sleep then, and it seemed like minutes later that I had to awaken and drag through classes, smiling at my friends and agreeing that, yes, I was excited that my friend would be coming soon.

In the afternoon, when he was *supposed* to arrive, I brought Ricky out of Simpson and into the daylight. I showed him off at lunch and, since I had no sports practice that afternoon, we walked together through the snowy woods. He'd brought a camera with him, saying that he wanted to have a photo of me in his room, so we took pictures of each other. Then we sat down to talk. Ricky had something to tell me, he said, looking serious, something that he'd been afraid to mention before. Now that he knew he loved me, however, he wanted no secrets between us.

Boys were so loath to share secrets that I rejoiced at the news. The night before I'd hated us both. Now I would have something to atone for it, some delicate intimacy to give the dark night meaning. We found a rock that jutted above the snow. There we sat until Ricky was ready to disclose his secret. If I could have, I would have placed my lips against his exquisite ears and sucked it right out of his brain, so eager was I. Instead, I declared my unshakable, unassailable love.

"Last summer, when I was back home," he began, "I made an awful mistake."

Ricky had a child.

I had not been expecting that. I'd left teenaged pregnancy at home, which was where his baby was and where it had been conceived. I had not thought that it would follow us here, not us ambitious ones, not the someday-we'll-give-it-back-to-the-community crowd cramming down Latin and calculus here in New England.

Ricky looked down at his feet and out onto the frozen water. The ice was pushed up, jagged and broken where it had frozen imperfectly. He seemed ashamed of the child's existence, and desperate for me to forgive him.

My forgiveness, I told him in a moment of candor rare for our romance, seemed entirely beyond the point. He looked at me strangely.

"So what is it?" I asked him.

"What's what?"

"The baby? Is it a boy or a girl?"

"Oh, he's a boy."

I had more questions that I did not bring myself to ask. Did the baby have his name? Was he healthy? Had he gone home for the birth? What was she doing for diapers? Did he correspond with her? Was he good to her?

"She doesn't mean anything to me," he said. "Never did. She said that she had protected herself. You know how some chicks are. It might not even be mine, but she said it was, and I know it could be. I'm not the kind of guy to lie about that. But, really, it was nothing. I hate to say it, but the fact is, she was nothing but a whore . . . and I was lonely. . . ."

I was trying to follow his reasoning. I tried to feel flattered by his concern that he might lose me through his confession. I tried to recapture my former appetite to share his secret. But the word he used, that word screams at me still across the years: *whore. She was nothing but a whore.*

And what was I? I thought, trying, but unable to keep from thinking it. What would I be next month if I turned up pregnant? I imagined myself big-bellied and barefoot, teeny-weeny little pickaninny braids sticking off my head, walking around the green lawns of a New England college somewhere asking: "Y'all seen mah Ricky anywheres? I's lookin' all over for mah man, me an' de little one what's a-comin."

I wondered if Nothing-But-a-Whore had had the good fortune to be awake while *her* unfortunate seed was being planted, but then that was too cruel for me to pursue, I thought. I had a boy here who was just plain manly. If I wanted 'em smart and virile, well, I'd just have to stop acting like I wanted something else. But I couldn't stop. I couldn't help but wonder what she'd be doing while I was curled in the big red leather chair in the reading room, my feet tucked under me for warmth, reading my latest James Baldwin novel or studying Paul's Epistle to the Ephesians.

The only seed that was planted that weekend was one of hate.

I began to hate Ricky a little that first night and a little more the next day, but I did not know it. I thought this new power and new entrapment, this new, complicated, busy denial were pangs of love. I thought that I loved this muscular young man with the sparkling smile. I could not understand why I was relieved to see him go, or why his ardent letters embarrassed me.

As winter progressed, the whole school went into rehearsal. The Master Players, the faculty drama troupe; the dance class; the Fifth Form religion classes preparing skits for our ethics unit; the dormitory houses producing short plays for the annual Fiske Cup competition. Simpson staged a brief adaptation of *Alice in Wonderland*. I was chosen to play the caterpillar by our student director, Janie Saunders.

Janie inhabited a large room on Simpson's most exclusive and private enclave, the third floor. Passersby never strode through on their way to the library. No one stopped in to pee in their toilets. Mr. Hawley and his big black dog (who was trained, rumor had it, to sniff out illegal substances) patrolled the third floor less frequently than they did our own. Most of the residents were Sixth Formers, or people like Janie who had the assured self-sufficiency of Sixth Formers. Girls on the floor lived in large rooms with three or four windows, instead of two, and they made entryways private by setting their bureaus perpendicular to the door. To get into their dens, plush with Oriental carpets, Indian wall hangings, rockers and coverlets, you had to walk around the bureaus. Years later, the Concord Fire Marshal warned that students would be trapped in their lairs in case of fire, and bureaus went back against the walls, but in 1972, the third-floor room of Janie Saunders, complete with its bureau barricade, breathed intimacy and exclusion, spicy perfume, makeup, and forbidden, fresh tobacco.

I had no idea what attracted Janie to me or why she picked me to play the caterpillar. I suspected as I always did that she mistook my skin for attributes of character, but as we came to know each other better, I realized dimly that she, too, was angry, and angry at St. Paul's School. She who had at first seemed so much a part of SPS—she was white, after all, and appeared rich, so far as I could see—she, too, felt herself an outsider, a rebel who didn't quite belong in any of the several white social tiers. She made fun of them. I liked her "perspective," as I called it.

Once I became a member of Janie's inner circle, my curiosity about my schoolmates was not satisfied but sharpened. I took to cruising the dorm at odd hours, just before sports or on Saturday nights, and poking about in the rooms—always on some pretense. I found myself drawn to the rooms as if standing in the middle, smelling it, reading posters on the walls and scraps of letters left lying on rumpled beds, would tell me some secret I had to know—and as if knowing the secret would somehow comfort me or make me strong. A few times when I saw a dollar or a five-dollar bill on the floor or tossed onto a dresser like so much trash, I pocketed it with shameful excitement. I fingered jewelry. Once I took a pair of earrings and cringed that night when I heard their owner howl and stomp around the house lamenting their theft. I felt the fine leather of their pumps and slipped my wide feet as far as they would go into the airtight duck shoes that kept their toes dry in the rain. As the house representative to the Student Council, I dutifully noted incidents of stealing; my old girl reported that a hundred dollars had been burgled from her room. That, I thought, was *real* stealing, done, no doubt, by some rich kleptomaniac, the same one who had probably eaten my cheese and crackers the week before.

Although these thoughts occupied my mind, I did not talk to anyone about them, not Annette or Grace or Pam Hudson or Janie or even Jimmy. I did not admit my growing difficulties in calculus. I did not tell anyone what had happened with Ricky. I couldn't. When I thought of the sex debacle, I was overwhelmed with shame. Like foam spread hastily over an offshore oil spill, my shame soaked up and protected me from the rage underneath. Only now and then did I see the results of that slick, silent anger: tiny moments of self-hatred like dead fish washed up on the beach.

Chapter Seven

Simpson did not win the Fiske Cup prize, and in a way, I was relieved. Sitting on the stage of Mem Hall, dressed in green caterpillar tights, sucking in the marijuana-flavored tobacco from the hookah Janie had procured, I was filled with fear that gave my four-minute performance a brittle chill. "Who are you?" I intoned through the wreaths of smoke. Everyone in the audience knew what I was smoking from, and I puffed the harder just to make sure that they smelled Janie's roll-your-own tobacco and not the sticky sludge at the bottom of the bong that made my throat burn and my eyes tear. "Who are you?"

I could barely keep my mind on my simple lines for the fear, and for the thoughts that flooded into my mind like stagelights. A fair girl, of course, played the title role, and I wondered if St. Paul's School would ever develop the imagination to accept a black girl as an Alice, or whether we'd be consigned forever to play animals, sidekicks, curios. Who was I, sitting, stomach sucked in desperately on account of the leotards, and my head, full of smoke and chemicals, screaming for air? Who was I, who pinched crumpled dollar bills from empty rooms in Simpson? Who was I who had experienced the pinnacle of romance and could only lie still as a corpse while the deed was done and weep with bitterness when it was finished?

"Who are you?" I asked from my great height on the table

that served as a mushroom. I asked it with no sympathy what-soever. I wanted her, this intrusive white child, to qualify her-self. Try it. *Who the fuck are you?* I liked her confusion. I liked my distance. I liked my own fear that called up for itself a protective and theatrical rigidity. It felt the most natural thing in the world, as natural as the subzero loneliness of the obser-vatory and the cold telescope bringing the Pleiades, like tiny crystals of ice, to my eyes.

It also felt natural to switch into overdrive for finals. I had enjoyed the feeling a few months before, and I liked it again. I knew that a few dazzling exams could make the difference, and I began, like some novitiate mystic, to try to induce in myself a state of being that would produce, if not visions, at least flashes of convenient insight. I read and studied. I took notes on my notes. I organized and reorganized, highlighted and underlined. I studied in the Schoolhouse and in the library, in my room and in the laundry room. I felt giddy and rigid at once, a state that I took to be the precursor to inspiration. I believed myself, finally, ready for exams.

On the night before my English exam, a boy who lived on Philadelphia's Main Line approached me as I walked down the drafty cloister from the dining room. Doug Ballard and I had had a couple of conversations about where he lived, and how to get there from my house, as if, I thought ironically, I were in danger of being invited.

"Lib," he called from a few steps behind me. "So, are you ready for English tomorrow?"

"I don't know." I slowed my pace to wait for him in case he had a good story to tell. We watched for teachers to crack around exam time, and in winter, what with the cold, dark weather, and the pace of work and sports, one of the new ones was bound to lose it. Doug had the mischievous look of some-one with naughty info.

"What's up with you?"

Doug jogged a few steps to catch up with me. We were even with the side door that opened onto the back path toward the Chapel and the woods.

"Listen," he said in a confidential voice. "Some kids are going out a little later to party. You really ought to come."

I began shaking my head.

"Wait a minute," he said. "It's just a few people. *Very* discreet. The worst thing before exams is to get all tensed up. Hey, you look tense. I just thought I'd ask."

It worried me that I looked tense. I had thought I was on the verge of enlightenment, but perhaps not. Perhaps this high-strung fatigue was exhaustion. I had exulted in my appearance that morning, thinking it my badge of courage. "I have read the word of the Lord our God until my eyes burned like the very fires of hell. . . ." The fact was, I just looked bad, ragglely, as they said in Philly.

I looked at Doug. He looked great. He and his crowd would sashay into the examination refreshed, their minds clear to write about all the ideas I was hanging onto by the hair of my chinny-chin-chin. *They'd do fine and I would miss out on my HH!*

"Sure," I said coolly.

"Really?" Doug seemed surprised. Immediately, I had second thoughts. Maybe he'd had a bet with someone. "Nah, Libby'll never party with you." Maybe I had just provided the evening's entertainment.

"Aw, cool," he added in the nick of time. "That's great." He seemed sincere.

"I don't have anything to give you for this," I said. Was I incurring financial obligations? I wondered. Would I be required at some time to pay back?

"Oh, please." Doug made a dismissive movement with his head, as if I had tried to hand him a dollar for driving me to the supermarket in a Porsche.

Off we went, out the side door of the cloister, along the

gritty, ice-packed path, down the wooden snow steps, across the bridges over the pond, and around the hockey rink into the woods.

Half a dozen students assembled in a tiny clearing and got down to business at once. Until the little pipe came round to me, I watched my new pals. They seemed not to mind. They were watching me, too. I decided to take a hit.

"No, you're wasting it all," someone told me.

"Take it like this—" Doug took the pipe from me carefully, so as to avoid burning his fingers on the hot bowl of the pipe or dropping it in the snow. He sucked in a mouthful of smoke, and then, instead of breathing out, inhaled again a few times, short, tiny breaths, as if to force the stuff deeper into his lungs. "Try it."

The figures around me (I could barely see their faces) were becoming impatient. Smoke that trailed off into the air could be going into one of them. I took a puff. The wad of weed crackled in the bowl. Heat from one inhalation traveled up the stem to burn my lips.

"Whoa!" someone said. "It's steaming now!"

"Great, give it here."

I handed the thing away and sucked in as Doug had done. Tears sprang to my eyes. Furry smoke curled at the back of my nose and throat. Should I choke it down?

"Suck," Doug whispered.

I drew it in until the burning went beyond my throat and into my lungs. I felt as if it would drown me to inhale again. I let out my breath in tiny bits, afraid that the burning would come back up.

"How's that feel?" someone asked me.

"Does it feel great?"

"I feel dizzy," I said. Actually, I felt stupid. I couldn't regain the rhythm of my own breathing.

The pipe appeared again. I had cleared up by now. If I could only get this thing right, I thought. Again it burned. "Hot lips," I croaked.

They laughed hysterically and lifted the pipe out of my fingers. I didn't feel like laughing.

Doug asked me for a cigarette. The get-high folkways had it that smoking a cigarette would extend the high. I passed cigarettes all around, thinking in that way to attenuate my debt for my two gulps of weed, and still hoping that the lovely feeling would kick in.

I did have a delayed response to drugs, after all. It had taken a double dose of anesthetic to get me under for my tonsil operation when I was a kid. As I stood with my feet in the snow like the Grinch on Christmas morning, I remembered the hospital in South Philadelphia when I was seven. I remembered dozing lightly and waking up in the hallway outside a big, noisy room with white lights. That was the operating room, I had thought. A tall black man was standing over me, ready to roll my bed into the room. He was wearing a green cap, gathered around the bottom and puffed out over his head like a Victorian night cap. People in the white room were laughing and talking together casually. I had never heard doctors speak like that. "Hey, wait a minute," the man yelled to the doctors and nurses. "This child is still awake."

"She is?"

"Are you awake?" he asked me.

I nodded yes. I had been trying to go to sleep like a good girl. I had lain "still as death"—one of my old relatives (I wondered who) had always used that phrase, and that's what I had tried to do. I had been able to doze, ever so gently, but not sleep. I couldn't get my thumb into my mouth. What had they done to my arm? I couldn't sleep without sucking my thumb. Then the man with the green gown and cap smiled at me and rubbed my cheek with his forefinger. It felt good to be rubbed. I was glad that he was not as angry as he had seemed when I'd opened my eyes. Then they gave me another needle. "You'll be asleep in a minute, sweetheart. Don't worry."

When I awoke, my throat hurt. It burned. I was alone in a gray room. Not alone, there were other crib beds with other sleeping children. I could look out a big window and see the hallway. A nurse walked by. I tried to call her to ask where my mother was, but she walked fast and did not look my way. I tried to put my thumb in my mouth, but I could not. The doctors had a cast on my arm. I looked at my hand. It was no more than a foot away from my face. I could not get it any closer. I began to cry. My throat felt as if it would tear open with each sob.

I snapped out of my reverie when I felt the hot pipe being pressed into my hand again.

"No, thanks," I said. "I'm afraid that that stuff just doesn't work with me."

"Doesn't work, eh? You look pretty wasted to me."

"Could be that it affects your body differently," one of the girls theorized dreamily. "Do you have other allergies? Food allergies? Respiratory?"

"Oh, yeah. I'm allergic to everything."

"Maybe that's it."

"Or maybe it's just that it's your first time."

"Lib! Is this your first time getting high?"

"Or not getting high."

They giggled a great deal.

"Well, if it's not doing any good, don't waste it. Pass it here."

"You are *so* greedy."

"Who's greedy? I haven't had any more than you have."

"One potato, two potato, three potato, four—"

"*Shhhhh.*"

We all went silent. "What?"

"I think I saw a match."

"Oh, God," I moaned.

"Shhhhh."

Even people who didn't party knew what a match in the woods meant: Sr. Ordoñez. He was thought to go walking in the woods to bust people. He carried his little package of imported cigarettes with him, they said, and you could avoid him if you watched for his match.

"What're we going to do?"

"Run!"

"Are you kidding? And attract his attention for sure?"

"I know. We'll hide."

I looked around desperately. The woods were bare.

"We'll be munchkins!" one of the girls said in a muffled shriek.

"Right!"

"Quick!"

"Down!"

"Under the snow!"

The girls were first. They lay on the snow and scooched around in it like huskies settling in for sleep. Then they scooped snow on top of themselves. Little mountains of snow piled up.

"I can't breathe!"

Giggles and puffs of steamy breath floated up from the mounds like spirits out of fresh graves.

I lay in the snow, too. I did not own a parka with a hood, nor was I wearing a hat. The snow nuzzled into my collar and melted down my neck. I felt it smash against the back of my Afro and work toward my scalp.

"I gotta go," I said. No one responded. I got up and shook myself. I do not remember whether anyone noticed my leaving or spoke to me. I only knew that I had to get out of the snow. It felt like a trap, like I'd be trapped for good. I had to get back to my house, back to my warm bed with my red-and-white afghan and the alarm clock ticking beside me.

I came to a creek that burbled under its icy coating. To cross it, I had to traverse two logs laid lengthwise over the place where the creek dropped a foot to empty into the pond. I was not sure that I could negotiate the crossing, but I could not summon the resources to look for another. I stepped onto the logs. The crust of snow slipped off one log to reveal a thicker crust of ice. My foot plunged over the edge of the log toward the creek. I saw sharp rocks in the creek bed, and felt my calf scratch against the log.

"You could die here," I said to myself. "See those rocks? You could slip over and hit your head and die."

I sniveled with shame. I slipped and crawled and clawed my way over and ran when I got to the woods on the other side. Again, the voice inside chided me. "Running now? Couldn't run back in the fall, when the sun was shining, and the ground was flat and the grass was green. Uh-unh. No. It was so hard to run, wasn't it? Bet you'll run now."

I'd sign up for Señor's class next year, that's what I'd do. So what if I was scared of him? Better to be scared of him in class than running away from him in the woods.

Back in the house, the lights in the hallway blazed at me. For some reason, I wanted to see Janie, but she wasn't there. I couldn't think what to do next, so I walked along the third floor and back, and then down to the second floor and back. I ran into Mandy Butler, and I noticed, with some resentment, how attractive and petite she was, how at ease with other boys and girls.

"I'm looking for Janie," I said.

"Janie? I think she may be down in Mr. Hawley's," Mandy said.

"Oh."

"His door was open, and I heard voices. I bet he's having a feed, or snacks or something."

"Oh. Maybe I'll go down." I did not feel capable of sitting

with a ginger ale on Mr. Hawley's rug and impersonating my-self.

Mandy peered at me. "Libby, are you OK?"

"I don't feel so hot. I just wanted to see Janie." Why was I repeating myself?

"Libby!" She got up close to me. "Libby, you are high!" Mandy Butler whooped. "That's a riot! *You* are high. You *are,* aren't you?" Tiny bubbles of spittle collected at the corners of her mouth.

"I guess so. *Please* stop shouting."

"Oh, my God! This is a *scream!*"

I turned to go down the steps.

"Don't go to Hawley's." She grabbed my elbow. "What are you doing? Use the back staircase. I can't believe this."

When I got to my room, Pam Hudson popped her head in from next door. "Where have you been? I thought you were going to come back and study for English. I've been here grind-ing away waiting for company. Were you at the library or—"

Pam's voice, husky and full of good-natured scolding, filled me with blubbery remorse.

"I'm sorry," I said.

"Libby, what's wrong?"

"I'm sorry. You were here waiting for me, and I said I'd be back to study English, and I should have been studying Eng-lish." When the tears came, they burned my eyes, and I won-dered why.

"Aw, don't get upset. Listen, don't *cry* about it." Pam could be big and maternal when she needed to be, what with that deep voice and those square white fingers and folksong-gray eyes. She came and sat next to me on the bed and put her arms around me. Pam always smelled as if she'd slept in her clothes, and I breathed in the scent of her, familiar and comforting as a sleeping bag. "Hey, look at me.

"Libby? Libby! *You are high.*"

"Oh, Christ, shut up, Pam." You could talk to Pam like that sometimes.

"Aw, Lib, now you're going to have a crying jag." She said it with true compassion even though she was laughing.

"Jag" sounded like a bad word. I'd heard it before, and I knew what it meant. "I've got to wash my face," I said, "and then we'll study for English."

She looked at me and laughed outright. "Go the hell to bed," she said.

"I have to brush my teeth first."

"The hell with your teeth. It takes years to grow a cavity."

Pam threw my clothes into a heap. I lay down and allowed her to tuck me in. "Take it," she said, as I tried to straighten my own bedclothes. "Just shut up for once and take it." She rubbed me a little and turned out the light.

"Pam," I asked, feeling my stomach churning, "would you wind my clock and set it for six?"

"What, are you crazy?"

"No, really, please. I've *got* to get up early."

"OK," she said in a singsong. "But don't blame me if you end up losing another clock." I'd ruined two clocks that year by chucking them across the room in my sleep. When I was sure Pam was gone, I listened to the ticking. It was like the loud tick-tock in my great-grandfather's room. I thought how I would have disgraced him, disgraced my whole family, if I'd been caught, suspended, expelled. The other kids would apply to Andover or Exeter, no doubt, but I'd be back home, on my behind. When the alarm rang, I awoke to find my thumb in my mouth.

Everyone was cleaning, girls filling and then overfilling trash cans with accumulated exam-week waste—papers, notebooks, hated texts, tissues, empty tampon and cookie boxes. I went to the refrigerator at the end of my short corridor to clear out my edibles: a dried-out piece of cheese that I refused to eat after some girl had had the temerity to nibble it, and the cold, miniature cans of pear nectar that my grandmother sent. (Pear nectar was never pilfered.)

I felt a resentful regret as I passed a pair of skis leaning against the wall between the refrigerator and Sara's room. I had lacked the money and the gumption to learn to ski that winter. Here I was in New Hampshire, and not learning to ski. I might never have another chance. I looked into Sara's room and envied her her long, slim legs and feet, their strength and skill.

I wished that I could be satisfied with what everyone said was a good, solid start at a St. Paul's career, but I couldn't. I wanted skills it took years to learn, experiences I would never have. I wanted to have what they had, just in case I needed it, like big vocabulary words.

I seem to remember the cold, solid knowledge that caught me occasionally during adolescence that the seasons came and went according to the rhythm of nature. What I missed I would never chance on again; some things were final; some experiences could not be shared. I thought of a girl back home who had become pregnant the year before and had had an abortion. We corresponded, and I saw her when we were able, but it was hard to talk sometimes.

"Oh, Libby, are you cleaning out the fridge?" Sara asked me. "It's so gross when people forget to do that."

I thought of the janitor of our building, cleaning up our messes. "If you dirty it up," my mother said, "best you clean it yourself. Nobody in this world was put here to wipe anybody else's behind."

That is how I remember that night. I felt trapped, driven

outside. I was certain that I could get free of the noise in my
head if only I could get outside where the cold black sky shimmered with familiar constellations.

But how certain can I be that on that particular night many
years ago Sara actually did park her skis against the wall by
the fridge? How certain that it was on that night and not one
of a hundred other clear, cold New Hampshire nights that I
went out to sit on the ice by myself? It was surely after my
failed attempt to find relaxation in a pipe or to fit in with kids
who played munchkins in the snow. I know that, because when
I sat on the Lower School Pond, I thought of them—and of my
shame at crashing through the iced-over creek bed, clumsy as
a white man on an Indian trail. I know that it was before we
went home, because when we returned in March the pond was
thawing, and the ice was breaking up. And I know that the
English exam was and is held near the end of examination
week.

Four years later, when I first read Shakespeare's sonnet 64
in a college English class, I attached that sonnet in my mind to
Sara's skis and to the night I have just described. In that class,
listening to my professor's enunciation, as crisp and as prom-
ising as a brand-new hardback, I also thought about my friend's
abortion, or her pregnancy, rather, and the teal-colored autumn
dusk when she told me.

> Ruin hath taught me thus to ruminate
> That Time will come and take my love away.
> This thought is as a death, which cannot choose
> But weep to have that which it fears to lose.

Those lines came back to me on St. Paul's anniversary weekend in 1989, the weekend that marked my fifteenth reunion.
They came to me after the annual parade, begun by the oldest
alumnus riding a golf cart and ending with the current grad-

uates, shouting and laughing and riding on each other's shoulders. (My husband dubbed it the seven ages of man.) The same sonnet came back to me the next day when I sat on the dais with the other trustees, who were older, whiter, and wealthier than I, and watched the black and Hispanic students in their suits and white dresses file past to receive their diplomas and toss a smile my way or a thumbs-up.

In this way I audit the layers of reminiscences, checking one against the other, mine against my schoolmates'. I trust the memory of my resentment of Sara's slender legs, the joy of perfect equipoise on the balance beam, the milky taste of Ricky's kisses. I trust the compassion a woman can feel for the girl she was. But it's also true that my memory is a card shark, reshuffling the deck to hide what I fear to know, unable to keep from fingering the ace at the bottom of the deck even when I'm doing nothing more than playing Fish in the daylight with children.

Still, I believe that after I cleared my foodstuffs from the fridge, I headed for the Lower School Pond. Behind me were the woods where I'd been the night before. In front of me the two Chapels jutted out of the snow: vigilant, haunted, and holy.

I walked out onto ice so thick that during a skating party earlier that term we'd burned a bonfire on it. I slipped at first, but it came back to me to pull my weight up into my hips and balance it there, to relax my shoulders and knees. The ice seemed to get darker farther from the banks. I kept walking because this was, after all, a game of chicken, but also because I wanted to see where the ice would turn black.

I had heard about black ice in the fall. Masters spoke of it with reverence. It figured prominently in nostalgic talk about the old days, back when St. Paul's was the first high school in

America to play ice hockey. The boys began their vigil in mid-November, hoping and praying for black ice, writing home about it.

The phenomenon they looked for is a clear, glittering ice that forms when it gets cold enough before the first snow to freeze the dark waters of the lakes. The surface acts like a prism to break winter sun into a brilliant spectrum of browns. Below, in the depths, frozen flora pose. Black ice is the smoothest naturally occurring ice there is, as if nature were condescending to art.

I went as far as the safety barrier, but not beyond. Tiny air pockets in the ice crackled under my boots. At the barrier I sat down on the ice, waiting for the cold dark to blow through and cleanse me. I wanted peace and clarity. I tried to think of Ricky, but other thoughts bubbled up. In a day we'd be boarding the buses, then the seven-hour train ride. Then I'd arrive at Philadelphia's 30th Street Station, that welcoming palace with the bronze angel with two-story wings holding the railroad's World War II dead in the form of a limp young man. Then home again to Yeadon, and the visits to my grandparents in New Jersey, and my family on Addison Street.

The stillness did not quiet me; I disturbed it. The woods quickened around me as surely as dolls and statues and trees had come alive in the dark when I was a child. Cold as I was, dark ice chilling me from below as the air seeped into my clothes, my mind conjured up the memory of two hot rooms in West Philadelphia that always smelled of liniment and some-times smelled of gin. I began to tell myself Pap's old stories. They began in the black night, too.

"Can you imagine how black? With not a light anywhere. So black and dark that women were sure to be home by nightfall, because they didn't know what could be out there. And men, too. *Big* men rushed to get in out of the dark and in their homes—where I should have been, but I had stayed and stayed and stayed. . . .

"But here, in this right hand, I carried a heavy stick, just in case. Cane grows up high, so I peered and peered trying to see, but there's nothing to see in the narrow rows, in the dark, so I listened. I first knew it was there; I knew it; and then I heard it as a rustle." He passed his fingers over the sheet and rubbed his dry feet together like the wings of a cricket. "Just a tiny rustle.

"And I stopped and turned in the darkness to face it. Then I saw it in the moonlight, crouched down low—a white dog, white-white, and I heard the growl in its throat. I felt the sweat in the small of my back. It moved toward me. I took that stick and threw! Hard as I could, I threw it."

He heaved into the air, shaking the bed down to its squeaky springs. When the bed was still, he growled out, with a voice held over from his once broader and younger chest:

"And it screamed! It screamed like a woman, and the moment it screamed, I felt the pain, felt it as if that cudgel had come back and struck me there, on my shoulder." Pap guided my hand over a knot of bone on his shoulder, like a fossil embedded in stone. "That was there the next morning when I woke up, and it's been there ever since."

I rubbed the knot each time to see if it had disappeared, or if the love in my hand might dissolve it.

" 'Poor Henry felt his blood run cold/At what before him stood—' "

" 'Yet like a man he did resolve,' " I answered him, " 'to do the best he could.' "

Pap nodded his approval at my recitation. Then he continued: "I learned," he said, "that some things *thrive* in the dark. One man, Horace, I think his name was, Horace and his wife were getting ready for bed, when a knock came on the door. The door was already shut for the night, and they had, like we all had, a heavy piece of wood that went across to lock it. So Horace called through the door, who was it? And a pitiful voice answered, the voice of a woman who had gotten caught out late and wondered if there was a man in the house to walk her home, just up the road, but she was sooooo frightened. So Horace told her to wait there, and he started to pull on his pants. And then, he was just lifting the bolt off the door, and his wife, it was, said to him, 'Horace, you better take your gun.'

"And then they heard it screech: 'Hah-haaaaaah!' the thing outside the door screamed. 'Your wife saved you!'

"Your wife saved you." He repeated the sentence again in a wee, small voice and laughed to himself.

We never said exactly what it was that was outside the door, but I had no doubt that it was a witch, some vengeful, rapacious spirit. I imagined that the spirits were always women, like the one who slipped out of her skin at night and flew around in the darkness. She left her skin draped over a chair by the window, as easily as others leave their lingerie. When her husband realized what was happening, he went to an old woman in the village and asked how he could keep his wife home with him, where she belonged. The old woman told him to pretend to be asleep that night and wait until his wife was gone. Then he was to take salt and rub it on the inside of her skin. So he did. Just before the following dawn, when the sky began to lighten a little, but the moon still shone white and silver through the window, the husband heard the rustling and then a shriek of pain as the wife tried to slip back in. "Skin, skin," she screamed, "ya na know me?"

I knew the stories so well that I daydreamed sometimes when he told them. I fell into a reverie in which I escaped from the city into a green wood, carrying with me my younger cousin and sister. It would be cold and clear in my fantasy, and the children would have to walk hard to keep up. I'd carry them toward the end, one in the front, the other on my back, until we reached a cave I knew, where we'd shelter from the cold. I'd build a fire to warm us, and keep us there, safe and quiet and gentle. I'd never beat them, and we'd grow up together, simple and strong.

At other times, I'd remember Grammom and her soft, salty food: The c'coo she made, a tomato-base fish stew, cooked so long that you could crunch the bones, poured over a green porridge of cornmeal and okra. Her kitchen had felt safe like my cave, safe from the women who now ran the family.

Now that Grammom was dead, Pap seemed to have lost his link to the women downstairs. He was Man to them, the only steadfast, ever-present man in their lives, as much symbol as flesh. He fixed things still, blind as he was, feeling the rotten wood where a screw no longer caught and fingering through an old tool box for a longer screw, the proper screwdriver and putty. But the family had grown out of his stories. Their womanhood seemed to be a taking off from the world of men below: as surely as they worked and worried to get a man and then build a home and a bed in it with him, so too did they seem eager to fly away. I had no doubt that if they could have, my mother and her sisters and my grandmother would have left their skins draped like pantyhose over their unsatisfactory furniture and floated up above us all: the men who never failed to oppress them; the children who'd ruined their beautiful bodies; and the boxy little houses fit to bursting with the leftover smells of their cooking and the smoke from their cigarettes, curling up and hanging just above our heads like ambition.

Pap withdrew from their magic womanhood, even as he praised it. Marrying them off, he said, was like throwing "pearls before swine." We said it to each other as we looked at the yellowing newspaper clippings of my twin aunts at twenty, caught by an admiring photographer at some social function or another, in identical broad-brimmed hats and fur-trimmed jackets.

If they allowed him to withdraw, however, and to ossify into a family icon, certainly he himself had taught them how and why: "There's a man whose daughter is standing at the top of some steps," he began, "and the child's name is Izzy. Now the father told the girl to jump down the steps, jump down to where he was. 'Jump, Izzy, jump,' he said. 'Papa's got you. Papa'll catch you.'

"But she's scared. 'I'll fall, Papa,' she says.

"But he answers her, his voice so gentle, so strong: 'Papa wouldn't let you fall. Don't be afraid. Come on, now, jump, Izzy, jump.'

"Finally the child gathers up her courage and jumps. She leaps toward her daddy's arms—and her father, he steps aside. The child falls, of course. She falls down on that hard ground, and it hurts. She's scraped herself, and it hurts. Her daddy helps her up and dries her tears, and she cries to him and cries and asks him, 'Papa, why didn't you catch me, Papa? Why did you let me fall? You said to jump, Papa, and I jumped.'

"And he says to her, 'Listen to me, Izzy, and listen carefully. 'Learn this this once and never forget: Trust no man.' "

We learned the lesson and whispered it into each other's ears like poison. "Jump, Izzy, jump," we said when one of us fell short, and then we laughed the grim, hysterical laughter of caretakers whom no one took care of.

I remembered Izzy and fashioned for myself the perfect pose. That was it. That was what I'd been trying to remember these months at St. Paul's School, the pose: I would be well-mannered, big-hearted, defiant, and, because a pose cannot resist great intimacy, at the center of all my posing, I would remain alone. I would trust no man.

. . .

I got up from where I sat, walked a little farther out onto the ice, and then circled round the pond and made my way to the bank. I was warm with exertion and reverie. Comforted by the old, familiar fears, I could go back again to face the new ones.

It did not occur to me that the ice I had been sitting on might not be the black ice I'd heard about. It wasn't. Black ice is an act of nature as elusive as grace, and far more rare. I did not learn about either until much later.

Chapter Eight

When I arrived home for spring break in March, no one else I knew in the Delaware Valley was on vacation. I felt as isolated in our home as a young housewife. I ate and slept and did housecleaning during the day. I also daydreamed, listened to the radio, and walked from room to room twirling my baton and smiling vacantly at familiar objects.

One day Mr. Hawley's end-of-term letter arrived with my grades. I had failed calculus. It seemed to him that I "simply met a difficult course . . . and did not really recognize this." He went on: "Thus, she did not try new methods of studying . . . such as extensive extra help. Mr. Shipman feels that she can pass calculus in the spring term if she takes some realistic steps in the studying of the course."

The rest of the groupmaster's report described my work at school as "excellent." Mr. Hawley wrote about gymnastics, the house play, my term on Student Council, and my other courses. The failing calculus paragraph, however, was longer than the everything-else-is-great paragraph. I felt aggrieved that he had not even mentioned my first High Honors in English; he had not even mentioned my other four Honors.

"The man says he thinks you can pass," my mother said in answer to my frustration.

"I don't want to 'pass.' " It was hard not to spit the words out onto the kitchen table. "I didn't go up there to 'pass.' "

I dared not say that I would almost prefer to fail outright than to scramble on my hands and knees for a P. The fact was, I wanted calculus to disappear. I wanted to drop it, reasoning that since I had taken one course more than was required, I had one to spare, so to speak.

The Vice-Rector disagreed. I would have to gather the strength to hurl myself at it once more. It was a two-term course. I could still pull it off. If only I could stand the pain of not understanding a little longer, the magic would happen. Understanding concepts was magic. It could come in drips or a glorious flood, but I couldn't tell. I had to keep studying and hold on. That was the hard part. Not understanding made me want to explode after a time. I promised myself that it would come like a difficult reading suddenly came, and then I'd have it.

It would happen as my father described falling in judo: "It's almost like religion," he said. "It's learning not to fight it. If you fight the fall, you lose. You always lose. But if you can just conquer the fear, you won't get hurt. You just fall."

We returned for mud season. The ponds were thawing. Water roared over the man-made fall by Simpson's front door. It foamed over the rocks and swelled the grass meadow below the quad. The paths were gritty with layers of sand that the grounds crew had spread over the winter ice. Grit and sand and mud encrusted the soles of our shoes. Tiny cylinders of dried mud popped from the eyelets and onto the floor when I laced my shoes.

Mountains of snow by the sides of the roads did not melt. The sun warmed them; the nights froze them; and they grew as hard and shiny as boils. Unexpected snows caught us by surprise at night, and freezing rains came suddenly, coating the trees and their tentative buds as if with shrink-wrap.

Despite setbacks, the buds on the tough little magnolia by the Schoolhouse fattened tenaciously inside their fuzzy pods, and the chickadees, their furry black-and-white feathers puffed against the wind, proceeded with their special springtime noise. It was a soft, surprisingly mammalian sound, delightful and disturbing. I, who was sometimes surprised myself these days by the sound of my own words (phrases and pronunciation I had worked to master now fell from my mouth spontaneously), I listened to these funny birds who did not sound like birds as if they could illuminate a mystery for me. They could not.

I continued to flail about in calculus. I cursed myself for ever having signed up for it. I cursed my teacher and made nasty jokes about him at table. I completed my homework assignments with grim determination, and emerged from each one as baffled as I had begun. I was just beginning to understand the ideas from the winter term, and it was already spring. I whipped myself into to a frenzy, hoping that pressure and panic would hasten learning, but with each new lesson, I fell further behind.

Grace's older brother was assigned to tutor me, and then I was released from classes altogether. "I am not sure that this will work," Mr. Shipman told me, "but at this point, I'm ready to try."

Four times a week I met with my tutor or with Mr. Shipman alone. Having escaped from the daily humiliation of class, I confused relief with progress. I remained just as far behind, only I didn't know it.

I chose crew for my spring sport. An old master named Mr. Church took us new girls out to the Lower School boat docks to learn the basics: how to get the boat off its shelf, down the dock, and into the water; how to step into the boat and strap our feet into the stirrups; how to position our oars in the oar-locks and where to grip the smooth butt of the oar. He taught us port from starboard, how deep to dip our oars into the water and how high to carry them when we pulled them out. Mr. Church had been in the Lower School for years, and he was as gentle with us as with twelve-year-olds.

Once we learned how to get the boat into the water without ruining the shell or hurting ourselves, he led us into the calm water. We rowed clumsily, scooping deep into the water or glancing the surface. At the beginning of the term we rocked and rolled. Chunks of ice floated by silently.

Once we knew the basics, they took us away from Mr. Church. Now we ran out to Big Turkey Pond, a mile from the gym. I detoured through the forest behind Upper to find a shortcut. I negotiated fallen trees and mud and moss. I took my occasional falls as just punishment for chiseling, and I chiseled nonetheless.

Sometimes I stopped running because I was tired, and because the woods were too animated to pound through as I was pounding through adolescence. Each day the snow retreated a little from the coldest, shadiest places. The mud softened, and the path became more treacherous. I came to know the working chipmunk holes, sunny bird roosts, and squirrels' nests, bulky as winter hats in the high branches of the hardwood trees.

My guilty afternoon pleasure made me greedy for more that spring, and so I left off studying now and then to read a short story or a poem that was not assigned or to skip the first half of Seated Meal so that I could steal away to the Lower School docks to watch the sunset melt into the tops of the pines.

I did not know that I was supposed to find in such solitary diversions moments of joy in learning so profound that I would cherish them into adulthood. I would have laughed just as my four-year-old daughter laughed when I told her that children grow while they sleep.

Ricky wrote to invite me for a weekend at his school. Over and over I asked where I'd be staying. I wanted a safe room, tucked far away, if possible, in an inaccessible den of some vigilant faculty member. That arranged, I came upon my inspiration for the term.

In biology lab someone mentioned a theory that the body needed as little as three hours to accomplish the daily physiological functions of sleep. About the same time I picked up another factoid, namely, that most people use only a small fraction—five or ten percent—of their brain capacity. It was like finding money in the road. I was so excited that I told everyone at the lunch table. They took the idea and worked it into a routine.

"You do the experiment, and then come back and tell us how it went," said Kenny.

"I gotta see this."

"Zombie time."

"She'll be sleeping standing up, like horses do."

Somebody made snoring sounds.

"Nah, guys, it's gonna be like this," said Anthony. He, too, was from Philadelphia. He was a tall, bulky boy who liked to tell stories and joke. "She doesn't half study anyhow, so what's the difference? You're gonna walk into class and do the same thing. No. Don't try to deny it. Check it out. This is how it is in creative writing—" Anthony pitched his voice to a high falsetto. " 'Excuse me, Mr. Ball, but I think with regard to the reading, uh, Life is like a leaf.'

"And Mr. Ball says: 'Now, let's think about the possibilities. Did the rest of you hear that? Repeat that please.' "

"I never said that!"

"Get out of here," Anthony said. *"I was there. I know."*

After lunch it was time for practice, and since they'd warmed to teasing me, they teased me some more about crew. The boys had come up with an entire routine about crew, which opened

with their whistling an old sailing song that was featured on a
TV commercial for men's cologne. "Yeah, matey!" they said
in unison. "Matey" was acceptable public shorthand for "fag-
got," a term they used frequently. "Down brothers" did not
row crew. Crew was effete. It did not translate perfectly in the
case of a girl, but (or maybe therefore) they ragged me anyway.
Then we went off to our separate sports: they to track and
lacrosse, and I to skulk through the woods to the distant boat-
houses.

I watched the back of the girl in front of me and moved my
body with hers. The oars dipped, and I listened to the sound
in order to hit the rhythm. Crouch and pull. Make the pull
smooth, hard, long as you could. The trick was to hit a balance
between thinking and not thinking. Once I'd gotten the oar
into the water just right, I had to stop thinking about it and
put my arms just there again, pull just so hard with my back,
slide with just the same force from my thighs and calves. It
took thinking about each part, and then letting go of the
thought so that the parts could work together. Now and then
I hit the balance. My body moved, and my mind was clear,
focused on nothing but the rhythm and the sounds of the oars,
the repetition, and Patty Glovsky's voice shouting hoarsely:
Stroke! Stroke! Stroke! Wood and metal and water made their
own sounds, and we were silent.

I was always astonished at the end of practice at how little I
had thought of my romance. Running back to the gym, on the
road, if I was not able to slip into the woods unnoticed, or on
the dappled trail, I did think of Ricky. I thought of his skin,
his nostrils, and his mouth. Some days I could not put the
features together and see his face in my mind.

When I visited his school, that forgetfulness amazed me.
Ricky had prepared for my stay: He'd found a fancy bicycle
for me. He explained its features and adjusted the seat. Together we rode on sloping roads that wound through the coun-

tryside near his school. We scrambled over hills and sped down, our pedals flying through tenth gear. We sliced through shadows, and I tilted my head to keep my eyes from tearing in the wind.

We rode about fifteen miles before I braved the disappointment that I knew I'd see in Ricky's eyes when I said I'd had enough. We rode back to his school underneath canopies of green trees, talking of bicycle design and our love.

"Well, what shall we do now?" Ricky asked me.

I wanted a bath, but that didn't seem the right answer, so I smiled and asked what he would like to do. Ricky took me on a tour of the campus and introduced me to friends. Then we ended up in the gymnasium, where we shot baskets. It was high time I learned to play basketball, we decided, and he tried to find my natural shot. We tried lay-ups, jump shots, set shots, free throws.

We meandered in search of yet more athletic equipment. Finding rackets, we played a little tennis and then went to dinner at the cafeteria. Dinner was clattery, noisy, informal, and followed hard on by the school dance. The inevitable man-sized speakers blasted out the inevitable rock music. It was violent music, and the dancing took on the aspect of hand-to-hand combat. We danced as best we could, but the music was against us, and elbows were flying. We left early. After cycling, basketball, and tennis, my thighs had begun to cramp anyway.

When I arrived back at St. Paul's the next day, I hobbled to the squash courts to smoke cigarettes with Jimmy.

"Are you sure this is the man for you?" he asked me.

"I don't know," I said. "Doesn't look like I'm woman enough for him, does it?"

I leaned against him and gave a moment's thought, as I sometimes did, to why Jimmy and I remained friends instead of lovers. I wondered whether or not I would say years later, as my aunties joked, that they had never been able to get excited over some of the nicest guys they'd known in school. "*Good* men. Good *husbands*. Loving husbands. Men you could talk to. *Good* fathers." And they'd laugh together and shake their heads over these good men who were now married up to the evilest women in the universe—and were *good* to the heifers. I'd never understood why they had not grabbed these men, or why they weren't sorrier to have lost them.

There was nothing of the comfort and easy, simple laughter of Jimmy's friendship in my angry, athletic love, nothing of the honest acceptance or joyful, everyday discovery. I asked Jimmy about it.

"Well, darling, don't ask *me*," he said. "We see how *I'm* doing in the romance department. At least you *have* a boyfriend. Now whether he's suitable is another question. Every girl I'm interested in wants me to be a brother. 'I love you like a brother,' " he mimicked.

I looked inquiringly at him.

"Not you, love. What we have is different. What we have is special."

I laid my head on his shoulder, disappointed and grateful.

It was at the end of that same week, I think, that I realized that the new calculus regime wasn't doing the trick. I pushed back my despair until the weekend. On Saturday night I went to talk about it to Mr. Hawley. His front door was closed. Virginia Deane was on duty that night.

My last contact with Miss Deane had been embarrassing. It had been she who had had to roust me out of my bed when the screeching fire-alarm bells had failed to wake me. In fact I had not awakened at all until I found myself standing outside in the snow, my bathrobe hung over my shoulders. How Miss Deane got me out of bed and down the hall, I never knew, but if anyone was up to the task, she was.

Miss Deane was hard-core crisp. Her hair, a combination of stark straight strands of black and white, gave off the sheen of pewter. She carried her no-nonsense, long-waisted New England body on hard-muscled little legs that tapered to fine-boned ankles. She smoked constantly and had a voice as low and as husky as a man's. When a girl in her group made varsity lacrosse or tried a new haircut, Miss Deane would smile widely and cry out with firm-bodied enthusiasm: "Oh, that's neat! That's just swell!"

At Miss Deane's that night a crowd of the house's most boring girls were assembled talking the most boring talk. I stayed for a quarter of an hour, and then excused myself to have another go at my math assignment.

I reworked the problem I had left and checked the answer in the back of the textbook. It was wrong again. Another wrong damn answer. I went back to the problem that my tutor and I had worked on earlier. I reworked that problem, checking my reasoning against his at each step. I could not understand it. I closed my notebook, and went to bed.

Grace was not in the bedroom. I tried to pray, but could only sing to myself:

> *Come ye, disconsolate*
> *Where-ere-ere ye languish.*
> *Come to the mercy seat,*
> *Fervently kneel.*
> *Here bring your wounded heart;*
> *Here tell-ell-ell your anguish.*
> *Ear-earth has no sorrows*
> *That Heaven cannot heal.*

I felt like somebody had died. Up above my head Miss Deane's shoes click-clacked from one end of the apartment to the other. The girls had left. I went upstairs and knocked on the door.

"You're back. I thought you were going to bed," she said as a greeting.

I did not know what to say to explain why I had come.

"Well, dearie, are you going to come in? Will you have something more to drink? Something hot? Or cold?"

Often Miss Deane directed us to her tiny kitchen alcove to help ourselves, but this time, I seem to remember, she poured for me. I sat on her couch, then on the floor in front of her coffee table.

"You look like you could use a cigarette," said Miss Deane, lighting one for herself and passing me the pack.

I was appalled to find that I was on the verge of tears.

"You really do have to find a way to get smoking permission, Libby, if you're going to continue this lousy habit."

I snatched the pack and lit one before she changed her mind.

"But you're not here to discuss smoking permission. So what's up?" Miss Deane sat on her couch. She seemed content to sit and wait until I could say something.

I began to talk about calculus, how I'd tried, how I'd studied, how I couldn't understand it, how Mr. Shipman hated girls (except two or three math whizzes). I bawled out my humiliation. She handed me a box of tissues.

"It is true," Miss Deane said, "that St. Paul's is just learning about coeducation. It's trial and error, like everything else. It's also true that some people in the community were more eager to admit girls than others. And it's true that some faculty members came here, frankly, because, for whatever reason, they preferred teaching in a boys' school.

"I don't know about your particular case, but you are not the first girl to feel that a faculty member has treated her differently from his boys. It's hard to know when it's really happening or when it's in our heads. There's nothing we can do about that right now—the fact of it or the way we feel—except to do what we're doing, and to be the best we can. You girls are the pioneers, and I'm afraid that this is what pioneers do.

"But that doesn't solve the problem of your particular course. What are you going to do about it?"

In one short speech Miss Deane had robbed my predicament of uniqueness and focused on my responsibility for action.

"And what if you fail?"

What if I failed? I looked at her. What answer did she expect? I couldn't fail. *I could not fail.* How could she sit there, smoking another cigarette and not offering me one, and just ask that? How could she?

"Libby, if you fail the course, you will go home for vacation, you'll fall asleep in your own bed, and you'll wake up the next morning. I do not doubt that it will be very painful. But you will be the same person. You will be you. Sometimes we feel as if something like this will destroy us. It doesn't."

I could hardly hear her. She was sitting across from me talking in the big, low voice, and I could barely pull the sound into my brain. "You'll wake up the next morning." What did waking up the next morning have to do with anything? She was as bad as the old ladies at church who prayed: "Lord, we thank you for waking us up this morning. You didn't have to wake us. You didn't have to breathe the breath of life and let us open up our eyes. But you woke us up, and we're thankful this morning." What was the point?

Miss Deane proffered a stern smile. "I have the feeling, Libby, that you've never failed anything before, and you think that that makes you who you are. It doesn't. We all fail something sometime. So you might as well get it over with and get used to the fact that life goes on."

I had to get out of her apartment. "Fix your face." That's what my mother had said after a spanking. "Fix your face."

She'd squeeze my chin in her hand and tilt my face up to hers, so close that if it were summer I could see the sun in the tiny beads of sweat that popped out in the downy hair over her lip, so close that I could smell her skin and breathe in the fury that rose off the top of her head like heat.

I fixed my face. I had gone to Miss Deane for hope. She'd given me a cannon blast of real life instead. I had not wanted to know what I now knew. She had treated me like a young adult, though. I held onto that. She had talked to me as though I could take it.

Whether I could or not was another story. Miss Deane's reality workshop came at a bad time. I had been sleeping little (in accordance with my experiment)—and my period was overdue. A few days after our talk I checked myself into the Infirmary with a fever, headache, trembling, and nausea. I could hardly move. I wanted to scream and cry. I wanted some act of violence—to do it or have it done to me. I wanted to stop dead. I wanted everything around me to stop. I hated the nurses for their questions. I wanted them to take care of me. I wanted to turn to vapor and rise up into the clouds.

I slept in the Infirmary nearly an entire day and arose to find evidence of friends' visits. Textbooks, complete with carefully noted assignments, were stacked on my chair. Little treats—a napkin stuffed with cookies from the Upper, a bottle of perfume, a nightgown and toothbrush—were piled on my table. Notes wishing me a speedy recovery were scribbled on loose-leaf paper and folded in half.

The nurse, a woman with one walleye and aggressive breasts, came in now and then to take my temperature. Once she woke me to drink a cup of bad tea and eat cold toast. I tasted the starch in my sleep. I dreamt of gladiator movies and Bible epics; slaves in fields; A.M.E. and Episcopal church services. I dreamt that I could speak fluent Spanish while Sr. Fuster and I walked arm in arm to the Upper for dinner. I dreamt of sitting alone at the red-and-white kitchen table on Addison Street trying to convince our Irish setter, Duchess, to eat the shiny green peas I had to dispose of before I was allowed to leave the table.

The nurse woke me once to eat Jell-O and ginger ale, and I dreamt of my great-grammom crossing the street from her house to bring me bowls of black-cherry Jell-O that shimmered like garnet. I dreamt that I was alone and unloved or that I was petted, pampered, cuddled, and warm.

When I awoke, really awoke, I went across the hall to the bathroom. Under the lights I looked puffy. I looked like women on the local news who have just been awakened out of a drunk and dragged from burning row houses. "Your son was killed, Mrs. Williams. How do you feel?" And those poor women would stand there stupefied, blinking at the TV camera. "Why don't somebody give them women a comb before they roll the film?" we'd say.

I looked as bad as I felt. There was a rightness to it. I scurried back to the safety of the stale, dark room with its awful reproduction of an awful oil painting of a tall ship on the sea. As long as I was there, as long as I was sick, nobody could force me to go on.

Attracted by my movement as a fox to its prey, Nurse bustled into my sickroom and made cheerful noises about my recovery. She used the medicinal we. "We must be better tonight."

(So that's why it was so dark.)

"Oh, we'll have you up and back to classes in just a few days. Now don't you worry."

Worry? I shook my head at her as I had shaken it at the ugly child in the mirror. I didn't want to go back to classes in a few days. I didn't want to be up and around. I didn't want to row anymore like a galley slave or work and work and work to clutch onto a moron's understanding of calculus. I didn't want to paint pictures that fell short of what I saw in my head, or open my heart to write papers that seemed, on later reading, nothing more than late-night babblings, pompous and glib. I didn't want to talk or sing or listen.

Then, as I lay in the dark, I felt a faraway grumping in my abdomen as if my organs were miles, not inches, below my skin. I had missed my last menstruation. Now I lay motionless to feel the glorious pain. My period was coming!

In the morning I greeted the day nurse as cheerily as she greeted me. "My, we *are* feeling better," she said.

I bathed and ate and read poetry and napped. I braided and oiled my hair. I brushed my teeth. I filed my nails and clipped my toenails and napped some more. I heard the three-minute bell for chapel, the hurried rumble of latecomers. I heard them leave chapel and file toward the Schoolhouse. I heard it all, and I napped and snuggled into the day's fresh linen and determined not to look into the mirror until later.

Later that day friends came to see me. I was touched and then annoyed by their concern. Janie convinced me to drop crew. "Honestly, you've got to drop something, and since they won't let you out of calculus—whatever prompted you to take it in the first place?—you'd better get out of crew. You don't like it anyway."

"I *do* like it."

"Oh, come on, it's just us, here. You know you can't stand it, Lib. You told me yourself you wanted to strangle the cox. And besides you can't swim. I don't know how you passed the test."

She was right. I had taken an indoor swimming course in the winter, but I still could not breathe properly to execute the crawl. All I could do was the sidestroke my grandmother had taught me once at someone's pool party. I didn't quite trust the sidestroke to save me in the icy waters of Turkey Pond, but Nana Hamilton said it would, and she was a swimmer—and a survivor. "I don't know why I tell you anything."

"Admit it. You hate it. You hate all the crewbies. I understand this mania for a well-rounded education, but you're obviously killing yourself."

"I am *not* killing myself. I just have mono. I could have gotten it from a water fountain."

I did not know that I had mononucleosis, but the doctor had mentioned the possibility and tested for it. It sounded better than admitting to my friends that I had exhausted myself as they said I would.

Janie had more news that day. She and I were among those nominated for class president. During the week, however, she'd decided to withdraw on election night—and throw all her support to me. I begged her not to.

"It's going to look bad," I said.

"Don't worry. This is all going to work out fine."

I was released from the Infirmary not long before elections. On a Sunday night I joined my classmates in the lecture room in the math building, our entire form, preparing to become Sixth Formers. The present Sixth Formers seemed much older than we. I couldn't imagine us growing to fit their places in one short summer.

I forget who conducted the elections—that is, who wrote the names in lists on the board, and who asked us if there were any changes in the nominations. When the question was asked, however, I raised my hand. I wanted to place my name under vice-president rather than president, I said. I wanted to run for the position I believed I could win. I'd never be elected president, and I did not want my name, after being rejected for president, to be swept into the VP category like a chip that had been sitting on a losing number.

Then, the person running the meeting acknowledged Janie.

She did it. She withdrew and "threw all her support" to me. I thought I heard signifying snorts from the black kids who sat on one side of me. I did not look at anyone.

Peter Starr was elected president. It made sense. Peter was scholarly and even-tempered. I respected his judgment. It was in his house that I had first met Mike Russell and Mr. Price. Then came the VP election. I went out of the room. When I walked back in, I was greeted by applause.

I had figured it was possible. In fact, I had even done a roll call in my head, but the fact of winning surprised me. The year before, Wally Talbot had been the first black president, but he had been impeached after he'd plagiarized a story from the *Reader's Digest.* I wasn't the first black, but I was the first girl, elected vice-president. It embarrassed me to receive so much attention. Then came the other elections, and it was over.

Some people congratulated me on the way out. But one student told me that the brothers and sisters had not liked the flim-flam I'd put Janie up to. White kids followed suit. I fixed my face to absorb their sidelong looks and congratulations.

When everyone was gone, I walked through the buggy night along the path that ran from the math building, down steps past the school store and snack shop, over the sluice by the power plant, and toward the meadow behind Simpson and the other buildings in the quadrangle.

Well, I had it, I thought, and much joy might it bring me. Fresh out of the Infirmary, I did not know how I would face anyone the next day; how I'd sit in chapel; how I'd go to classes or walk along the grounds. How had this happened? Janie's bad timing had not helped, but I could not, even though I wanted to, blame her. Now I stood falsely accused, ironically, of duplicity in the service of crude ambition.

Bread on the water comes back tenfold. You reap what you sow. You can tell the tree by its fruit. Grammmom's old saws came winging through the years like supernal punishment.

Certainly, I had gone into this election with honest goodwill, but what of the rest of my life at St. Paul's? What of all the girls in Simpson for whom I had feigned more affection than I'd felt? What of cut corners, unread homework assignments, unrun laps? What of my secret hatred for my gymnastics coaches? Had I not slandered the woman as a "dyke" and made fun of the way the man's haircut zoomed out over his big ears like the helmet of a bloodthirsty Visigoth? What of my insistence on smoking in my room after Mr. Hawley had told me time and again that flagrant rule breaking made his job harder, tore at the fabric of community in the house, and encouraged younger girls to do likewise?

This general social rejection at the moment of triumph was precisely what I had feared. It was like the horrible scene in old novels when the parvenu appears overdressed and unchaperoned—whom would she know to invite?—at afternoon tea.

Hadn't we read in religion about people making their secret fears come true, like a kid who walks along a path saying to himself over and over again: "I'll fall on that rock. I'll fall on that rock. I'll fall on that rock. I'll fall. I'll fall."

"Guess what, class?" Reverend Ingersoll would say. "Boom!"

Over and over and over I had said to Jimmy, and to other friends, that I did not want to be trapped in one world. I wanted to be black, to be part of our group, to draw nourishment from it and give back, and yet I wanted to be free to come and go. How stupid I had been! How arrogant! In the process I had never loved well enough, I thought. Why else was I so alone on the dark path? *You reap what you sow.* Having no other outlet in my repertoire, I began to cry.

"Oh, God, don't cry. It's all right."

Tommy Painchaud had been walking behind me. "Don't listen to that stuff. Who says everybody's thinking that? I heard what they said."

Painchaud was a townie. He spoke in a nasal New Hampshire accent, and he was friends with several of the black guys. He played ice hockey but in some respects, he, too, was an outsider. He stood beside me with a boy's awkwardness while I cried.

"I didn't put Janie up to it," I babbled. "I didn't. She told me she was going to do it, and I asked her not to. I didn't try to pull anything on anybody. I wouldn't even have wanted it that way. . . ."

"Who the hell cares?" Painchaud breathed in my anger and exhaled into the night. "As long as you know you did right, who the hell cares?"

"I can't face them." I thought of the class officers' seats in Chapel, two on one side and two on the other side of the aisle, facing the entire school body. How would I sit there next year, day after day?

"You've got to face them. And when you do, it'll all go away. It will. Listen. People here always got to have something to talk about, and if you do anything different, they're going to talk about you. Everybody always talks about everybody. That's one of the things that's wrong with this place. But in a week, it'll be something else."

I did not know which consoled me more—knowing that Painchaud cared enough to stand on the path and talk to me or realizing suddenly that my supposed perfidy was not upper-most on everyone's mind, and certainly would not remain so. I remember wanting to touch Painchaud, but being afraid to. I thanked him repeatedly and cried some more. Between the two of us, we found something for me to use to blow my nose.

"I think you'll make a great vice-president," he said, "although I don't really know what a vice-president does."

The next day I arose early on purpose. The spring morning smelled wet and fresh. Midseason bulbs were pushing up through the heavy soil, and evidence of the grounds crew was everywhere. I breathed in moisture and the unhurried time that

rested between the chimes for seven-forty-five and three minutes of eight. I saw an entirely different crowd of people that
morning. Unlike the students and faculty who rushed to chapel
as the warning bells tolled, these people looked well rested.
They stopped to chat with each other and with me.

"Congratulations!" several of them called to me as we passed.

"I heard the news. That's great!"

I had not expected the gentle, tentative surge of gratitude I
began to feel—not just for the election, but for St. Paul's School,
the spring, and the early morning. I needed the morning light
and the warbling birds. I needed to find a way to live in this
place for the moment and get the good of it. I had tried to hold
myself apart, and the aloneness proved more terrible than what
I had tried to escape.

Room requests for the following year came due at the end of
the spring term. I asked Alma Howard to room with me. Alma
laughed easily; she did not hold grudges; and once, when a
couple black girls in Middle House had decided to punish me
for telling our guys about the good time we girls had had at a
dance at a boys' school to the south, Alma had refused to join
in. I remember that I did not know how to tell her how grateful
I was. No wonder she was surprised when I asked her to room
with me.

"You're asking me?" she said with characteristic bluntness.
"I don't know. This is kind of a shock. Don't take me wrong,
now. I just got to think about this a little. Hooking up with a
roommate is a big step." I don't remember whether she thought
for ten minutes or a couple of days, but when she decided to
room with me, it was with enthusiasm. "That'll be great."

I was as pleased as if I had arranged my own marriage.

We decided to live in North Upper, one of the three houses
over the dining commons. The three connected Upper houses,

which had been the exclusive domain of the older students in the boys' days, had retained their reputation. Upper was profoundly cool, and North Upper had just been declared a girls' house.

Each day there were more arrangements to make for the next year. We chose our houses and our courses. We began planning to take advantage of the Sixth-Form academic privilege: independent-study projects. College advisers called a meeting of our form and then scheduled individual appointments with us. Class assignments accelerated. We wrote final papers, took end-of-the-term tests, and rushed to complete research assignments. Everywhere—in the music building, in Mem Hall, in the Chapel—students rehearsed for Anniversary Weekend. Flower beds of big, bright annuals appeared, diminishing the beauty of cardinal flowers that bloomed on knee-high shrubs along the wood paths. Preparations for exams, for the next term, for college, for bright and shining futures seemed endless. Preparation was our life, and it was startling when, on the first Saturday in June, the main gate actually swung open to admit the handsome cars to drive in under the boat-club banners: maroon and white for the Halcyon Club, royal blue and white for Shattuck.

Once again parents arrived, but this time others came, too— whole families, children, and old people. Young men, recent graduates, appeared and headed for their bivouac in the gymnasium. Students and alumni fund-raisers gave speeches. There were special lunches, teas, cocktail parties. People opened the tailgates of late-model station wagons to reveal neat and not-so-neat hampers of food and drink. Young alumni drank beer conspicuously. Older ones toasted each other with champagne in plastic stemware.

On Saturday afternoon, long, horse-drawn wagons called barges loaded up the school's best rowers outside the gymnasium and drove to Turkey for Halcyon-Shattuck races. After the races, athletic prizes were awarded in a ceremony under the flagpole by the pond. Saturday was noisy, crowded, celebratory. Hundreds of people I had never seen behaved as if our School were their second home.

On Sunday morning the Chapel bells rang out hymns. The bells had never chimed so merrily. Song after song pealed out, and then suddenly, we were walking fast in our dresses, the heels of our pumps sinking into the soft grass, to bleachers set up on the green between the Chapels and the pond. On the hill behind us, the faculty and trustees in their black robes and caps stretched out in two lines, and hidden behind a tall hedge on the facing rise, the Sixth Formers: boys in ties and jackets, girls in white dresses, talking, laughing, adjusting each other, waiting for graduation to begin.

The Sixth Formers graduated, as St. Paul's School Sixth Formers do, at two o'clock on the first Sunday afternoon in June. At three-thirty, according to custom, they were to be gone. The grounds were empty without them. We moped around trying to fill up the space. Girls who had gone out with Sixth-Form boys dragged themselves about as if their limp bodies were merely vehicles to carry their tearing eyes. We Fifth Formers strutted self-consciously, telling everyone who'd listen, mostly each other, that we were the Sixth Formers now, and wondering how we'd make it without so many people we already missed. A school of nearly five hundred was suddenly a school of three hundred and ninety. At cafeteria supper we were not enough to fill the tables. After dinner our voices sounded high-pitched and thin in the common room, like a choir whose bass and tenor sections have been kidnapped. Even our houses seemed vacant and grubby. We picked through the untidy piles of Sixth-Form leavings in the halls. We sat on chairs and ottomans and bits of rugs we'd bought from them the weeks before, and instead of feeling important, we felt dull and aggrieved to have yet another week and a half of exams to go.

I watched Lee Bouton graduate, and I cried to think that she was the first black girl ever to receive a St. Paul's diploma. I remembered one afternoon when we'd soaked in adjoining perfumed baths and pretended that St. Paul's did not exist.

I thought of José Maldonado, who had teased me—and so often hit the mark. "I don't know why you keep trying to be such a brainiac," he once told me. "You go out in the middle of the night to look at the stars with all your Embryo Joe buddies. It's not good for you. No, do not laugh. This is serious. I want you to look at the dudes you've been hanging out with. Have you noticed that they have big heads and little bodies? Do you want to be like that? You want to be a brainiac? Well, hey, just make sure you don't end up getting more than you bargained for."

When the spring term ended, I had not achieved brainiac status. I brought home not one of the awards I had coveted that year, but a home-study packet from the math department instead. I had indeed failed calculus. I convinced myself that when I was home I would somehow be able to do by myself what I had been unable to do with the help of a tutor and my teacher. After all, I had failed the final by only a few points.

I hurried to bury my bitterness in a flurry of activity. I'd get on with summer. I ached to get a job, make some money, learn to drive, to leave New England boarding school and step back into an all-American adolescence while I still could.

Chapter Nine

I got a job as a waitress at a diner. My father awoke early so that I could learn to drive his old car on my way to work. I ground my way through the gears of the Peugeot he had bought with cash when I was three, and the summer rushed by, measured out, as it had been the summer before, in tips against the money I wanted to have saved by September.

Waitressing at the Hearthglow DeVille provided an antidote to school life. I worked with white waitresses and black cooks. Nobody talked about "past achievements and future hopes." My bosses told me that they'd had one other black waitress, and she hadn't been able to handle the work. They took my stubs off the spindle by the register to double-check my addition. A few customers told me with a leer that they preferred dark meat. I was back to black and white in America as I'd known it before, with none of the confusing church-school rhetoric about community sharing. Everybody figured he had the other side figured out. I wasn't able to think so with the same certainty any longer.

Our dishwasher was a punch-drunk old man who had once been a fighter. His face showed the punishment it had taken. His speech was slurred, and he jabbed at the air, like some caricature on the stage, each time the cooks rang the bell for us to pick up our orders. When business was slow, one cook named Booker would hit the bell just to amuse the assembled company. Then he would cover the bell with his hand so that none of us waitresses could hit it again and stop the old man from dancing around, hooking, dodging, punching, in the small square bounded by the dishwasher and conveyor belt.

"Oh, Booker, stop it," we'd say.

Booker would giggle, his eyes red from the marijuana he ducked outside to smoke on his breaks, and when he had had his fill, he'd move his hand from the bell. One of us would hit it and, for the old man, the round was over. He'd resume stacking dishes as if nothing had happened.

The cooks played other pranks to amuse themselves. They initiated me by switching the foods on my orders. Salisbury steak with mashed and carrots and broiled fish with French fries turned into Salisbury steaks with fries and fish with string beans and mashed. During my first weeks, when I was learning to balance four plates on one arm and learning the rhythm of restaurant service, I would stomp into the kitchen, grab the plates by my checks, and stomp to my tables, only to find the customers calling me back after a few bites.

"Check your orders," a woman named Elaine whispered in my ear as I passed her. "Check every goddamned potato. They're playing with you."

It astounded me that black cooks would so bedevil a black waitress, the only black waitress at the white suburban restaurant. I became wary of them and alert. Booker would ring the bell for me, and then click his tongue against his teeth. "Oops. I thought your steak was done. What'd you want it? Medium rare?"

"Yes."

"Sorry, not quite yet. But it'll sure be nice to watch you walk out again."

I had to learn to ignore the noises when I walked out the swinging doors with a swish; how far to trust the older women, women who were not making extra money to buy books, but were supporting families; how to serve different customers. There were talky ones who'd hold me up while other people squirmed to have their orders taken; four-dollar-a-plate gourmands who asked whether the French fry oil had been changed that day, whether the cucumber salad was fresh ("Ask him what he expects for three ninety-five," Elaine said. "Tell him to go buy a cucumber and sit in his car and eat it."); the Friday-night polka crowd with their hoop skirts and cowboy string ties. They arrived in slews of eight or more, each ordering groups of side dishes ("Now, let's see. I'll have macaroni and cheese and an order of cole slaw and a small salad with French on the side. And don't put them on the same plate. I can't stand to have all that stuff together. I'd like the salad first, and I'll have tomato juice with lemon with that, and then afterwards, I want apple pie with chocolate ice cream and a cup of coffee. No, make it Sanka or I'll be up all night.") —and then left a quarter under each pie plate.

Hearthglow was washing my head clear of St. Paul's.

One night after the dinner rush, just when the teenagers were coming in and before the polka people, one of the cooks, the broiler man, told me that if I wanted more butter, I had better go into the freezer and get it myself. That wasn't his job. I did not answer him, but went behind the cooking area down the narrow hall where the walk-in freezers were lined up like coolers in a morgue. I didn't think it was my job, either, but this man was mean-tempered. I was afraid of him, and he knew it.

I opened the big lever to the middle freezer and stepped in. Plastic packages of meat were stored on shelves. On the floor were boxes, as big as moving boxes, filled with little containers of half-and-half, butter, French fries, and vegetables. I browsed the freezer quickly, as if it were a dictionary that I had opened to look up a word, only to find a delicious storehouse of other words waiting to be read. Then the door closed behind me.

I did not turn around until I convinced myself that there must be a lever on the inside. Surely, freezers were made that way. They had to be. Doors bumped closed by accident all the time, I thought, and the freezer companies couldn't pay the damages that would be filed by families of suffocated workers. I breathed deeply of the frosty, food-laden air. It smelled of meat and frozen blood. When I turned, the cook was standing behind me.

"I was wondering when you'd look around," he said.

"Open the door."

"You got your butter yet? Don't look like you got what you came here for."

I reached into the box and picked up a few pounds of butter.

"That's not going to be enough," he said.

I knew it was not enough, but I wanted to have one hand free.

"I'll get more later."

"I didn't get what I came for, either," he said. He moved the toothpick in his mouth from one side to another, and then took it out. "You scared?"

"Just let me out. I got tables waiting. I got money to make."

"You ain't making no money here. This here is chump change. You *could* make some money if you put your mind to it." He grinned.

"You know what I'm going to do? I'm going to walk past you, and then I'm going to open that lever, and I'm going to act like this has all been some kind of joke. So far, it's a joke."

"Don't threaten me."

"I'm going to scream now."

He laughed. "Go ahead."

It was obvious that no one would be able to hear me.

"They're going to be missing us."

"Ain't nobody missing nobody. All they're doing is running around simple like they always do."

He reached out and grabbed my arm. I watched his face. I watched where the sweat had stopped dripping and had cooled on his head, nearly bald, but covered with a fine growth of slick, black hair. He was much taller than I, and he liked to roll up the short sleeves of his white T-shirt to reveal his knotted biceps. I watched his face, because I knew that I could keep the panic out of my eyes. I waited for him to move again, gambling that I'd be faster than he, that I could throw myself against the lever and shout over the kitchen din.

He held my arm so hard that I dared not move it and expose my comparative weakness. He put his other hand on my face and swept it down my body. I wanted to hurt him. I would wait, and I would hurt him somehow.

"Let me go."

"You too good?"

"Get your motherfuckin' hands off of me."

"Don't talk like that." He gave my torso another squeeze and opened the door. "You got a nasty mouth sometimes," he said, holding the door ajar. "You'd better just make sure to keep it closed."

I couldn't talk when I got out of the freezer. All I could do was put the butter out, pick up my plates, and serve my customers. I couldn't even talk to the other waitresses.

When my shift finished, my father came to get me. I drove the car badly. I stalled three times trying to get into first gear and crest a hill at a stoplight. My father told me about his experience stalling out once when a police car was behind him. I listened to the story he had told me before, and I soaked up the safety of being in the car with him.

The next day I arrived at work early and spoke to the manager. He was a sloppy older man with a belly that oozed like lemon curd over his belt. He tasted each dish every morning. By noon, the corners of his mouth and his nubby short-sleeve shirts were stained with the day's specials. He looked worried as I told him about the cook who had trapped me in the freezer, and I knew he was worried about having to do or say anything that might upset the cook. He, too, was afraid of the man, and I knew from experience that he hated to hire new people. He told me to watch myself, and to make sure that I did not provoke the cooks. There had been only one other black waitress at the Hearthglow Diner, he said, and she hadn't worked out, but "you're doing good," he said. "We like you."

I waited through the day for his bosses to come in. They were an Italian couple, a big, fatherly man named Jerry and a tiny, sharp-faced beauty who wore long dresses and acted as the hostess for the fancy DeVille side of the restaurant. It was the wife who chided us and insisted that we hem our dresses so high that none of us could bend over to wipe a table properly. But it was Jerry who came up with practical solutions to the daily whining and squabbling. He switched day schedules for a woman who needed to take care of a sick child. He moved the toaster to a separate table so that there would be enough room for us to work during the breakfast rush.

I found a way to get Jerry alone. He looked at me with his face troubled, annoyed, and sympathetic. He asked me whether the cook and I had ever dated. He asked me whether or not I had messed around with any of the other men. I did not feel indignant when he asked me these questions, so intent was I on telling my story and making him listen. I answered no solemnly to his questions and swore allegiance to my boyfriend (who I said was in college).

The next day the broiler man was fired. No one in the kitchen spoke about it. No one switched my orders. No one spoke one word more to me than necessary. In a few days the waitresses began to ask me questions. I answered them honestly, but briefly. Then one day, when we were particularly busy, and two kitchen helpers had called in sick, Booker cursed at a new woman (she didn't last long) who had made a mistake. He took the plate of food he had prepared according to her check, but that she now wanted changed, and he threw it in the garbage. "Now I tell you what you do. You go over there and write it like you want it, and then you put your check right here at the end of the line and wait for it, just like everybody had to wait while you were in here fucking up the program.

"Shit!" he said to no one in particular as he grabbed the next check. "I'm burning the fuck up back here. Got no help whatsoever. Fifty pounds of rotten potatoes stinking me out. She's in and out like to drive a man crazy, and I can't even sit down for a drink of water."

I poured a large glass of soda and ice as I had seen Elaine do, and reached over the steam table to put it on the cutting board. Booker turned around in time to see me, and he took the glass from my hand. He drank the entire glass down noisily, and stood for a moment with his head tipped back.

"Why'd you get the man fired?" he said, looking up at the ceiling.

"He got himself fired. I didn't get him fired."

"Nah, don't give me that. You went in there and talked to the Man."

"So I talked to him."

"Hey, well, check it out. The man's gone, ain't he? He was only playin' around."

"No, Booker. *You* play around. He wasn't playing. Do you go around locking people in freezers?"

"Hell, no, and I guess, from the looks of things around here, I better not start or I'll be out of a job." He laughed to himself. "He was an evil brother anyway. Hey," he called as I turned to go. "You can do that—" he said pointing to the empty glass—"whenever you like." For a brief moment, he grinned, with no irony, mischief, sarcasm, or boredom. He looked at his checks and moved mine to the front of the line.

"Oh, Booker," I said, "don't do that."

"Why not?" he asked. "I've moved it to the back plenty enough."

I visited Ricky that summer in Schenectady. I met his family. We took the usual photos. I played with his younger brothers and talked to his mother, who welcomed me warmly and made us banana pudding for dessert.

Ricky and I had the familiar tussle about sex. He gave me instructions to leave the door to his brother's room unlocked, and I insisted that I did not want to be sneaking around in his parents' house at night. We visited Niagara Falls and climbed to the top of the hill over the falls. There Ricky gave me a tiny diamond pendant necklace. He asked me to marry him, and I agreed, but all I could think about was that somewhere in his neighborhood, somewhere in the store where his mother shopped, a young woman was buying diapers while we planned smugly for medical school. Somewhere in the park where he wanted to kiss and I let him, because there seemed no way not to, a girl my age would be rolling a stroller while I was filling out my applications to a careful selection of Ivies.

I returned home dispirited by my lack of integrity. I had no intention of marrying Ricky; I had no intention of dating him anymore, but I had not had the guts to tell myself while I was there in Schenectady eating his mother's banana pudding, and I'd certainly not had the guts to tell him. Soon after I got home I threw the pendant into the trashcan.

"Oh, my Lord. Well, I guess that one's over," my mother said. She fished the pendant out of the trashcan and told me there was no need to take my anger out on a harmless little diamond.

"I don't want it," I said.

"Well, you can keep it. It's just a piece of jewelry."

"It's not a piece of jewelry. It's an engagement necklace. It's like those rings they put around pigeons' legs to identify them."

"Oh, for crying out loud, it's just a necklace. Where do you get that kind of talk? It's a perfectly lovely little necklace."

"I don't want it. And I don't want these around." On the kitchen counter was a double frame with the pictures that Ricky and I had taken of each other on that first, fateful weekend at St. Paul's. He had sent the framed photos to my mother for Mother's Day—a far more impressive present than I had sent her myself.

"Now wait a minute, wait a minute," my mother said, laughing. "Just because you're through with that boy doesn't mean you have the right to go throwing away my pictures. If you don't want the necklace, fine. *I'll* wear it. It's cute. But I can't just change up in an instant. You bring the boy here, and tell me this is it, he's the one. You get me to love him, too, and then a few months later, you're through and I'm hurt."

I told her about the girl in Schenectady who'd had his child. I told her that he'd called her a whore.

"Well, now, that's a shame," my mother said. "You just can't tell, can you? Seems like you just can't trust 'em sometimes, doesn't it?"

In time she moved the pictures upstairs to the third floor.

Soon after, as if he had radar to detect it, Booker asked me how my "college boy" was doing.

"All right," I said as I loaded my arm with plates and pivoted toward the swinging door. I placed my heel on the threshold with my foot at a forty-five-degree angle to the door as I had a thousand times before, and pressed my foot down against the door to flip it open. For the first time since the beginning of the summer, I slipped. My old-lady shoes with the built-in arch supports, on which I had spent fifty of my waitressing dollars—I had never imagined that shoes so ugly could cost so much—were slick on the bottom from a spot of grease on the floor. I recovered myself, but just barely, and as I lunged through the door, I heard the calls behind me for a mop.

I stayed out on the floor a long time, since all my customers, it seemed, had come in at the same time, and all of them needed their orders taken at once. When I came back in with my several checks, I was ready with a line of patter. The fact was that Booker hated to read, but he could keep a restaurant full of orders in his head. Usually when he saw us lining up several orders at once, he'd shout: "Talk to me."

This time he did not, so I began, "I'm ordering: This looks like a bunch, but they're all nice and easy. . . ." Then I told him what the customers had ordered in the order in which I wanted to receive the food. Uncharacteristically, Booker said nothing. When I came back to pick up the plates, he asked me whether or not I would like to go out with him that weekend on a night we both had off. Each of us was surprised when I said yes.

My mother understood more quickly than I that I wanted a date, a normal, local, friendly, working-class date. I disputed, almost by reflex, that my date with Booker had anything to do with my unilateral breakup with Ricky. She smiled her crooked smile. Then she asked me how old Booker was and told me that I still had to be home by midnight, prep school or no prep school. My father, who seldom had anything to say about my boyfriends, made it clear that he did not approve. I could not figure out why.

Booker did not have a car, and I was not allowed, by state or family law, to drive at night, so we arranged our dates according to the schedule of the bus to Philadelphia.

Once he took me to a card game in a house in West Philly. We proceeded through the first floor, through small groups of watchful people, to the basement, where the game was in progress. Booker played poker. I watched and helped him bet. At some point in the evening, someone pulled a gun and put it back again. We left soon afterward to find safer amusement and ended up at a bar downtown.

"I don't want to get carded," I said at the doorway.

Booker scanned my face and body with his small, quick eyes. I was sixteen, and I felt it. I had told him and everyone at work that I was eighteen. The drinking age in Pennsylvania was twenty-one.

"You won't get carded," Booker said. "Besides, you don't have to worry about nothin'. You're with Booker."

Men, I was discovering, had a habit of saying such things, as if their saying them made them so. I laughed at him, and he took my laughter—with what feelings I do not know. I did know, however, that I had a ten-dollar bill shoved in my bra, as my mother advised. "Take your carfare. No matter who you're with, take your carfare—and a dime." Since I had no pockets, the dime rested in my shoe. I felt it slip underneath my toes as we stepped into the portal.

At the bar, Booker remarked on how short I was sitting down. He was six feet tall and long-waisted. I was five-five and short-waisted. He liked women with long legs, he said. The only problem with them was that you could hardly see their heads when they sat down at a bar. Booker bantered on. I remember that I did not talk much—he commented on it—because I had so much to do to watch. The bar made me wary.

I had no idea what to order when the bartender came to us. "CC and water" came to mind. That's what Jane had ordered the night when her father had taken us out to dinner at a restaurant in Concord. The waiter had asked for our drinks, and he'd turned to us. "What would you girls like?" I was deciding between ginger ale and Coke when she'd let fly with "CC and water." Jesus, God, I thought. Bad enough we were happily smoking up a storm right in front of the man's face, but drinks!

Booker ordered a beer and shot of something and proceeded to tell me about boilermakers. He stoked his boiler. One after another of the neat little combos came, the amber liquid in the thick shotglass, and the big, sweating mug of beer. Booker was showing off for me. He asked about my college boy, and I evaded. He asked about my college, and I described St. Paul's, concerned at first to omit any telling secondary-school details, and then realizing that there were none that he would recognize. He told me about getting high in Vietnam, and about how a buddy of his, a guy who was blind in one eye and had lied about his blindness to accompany Booker into the service, had carried him a mile and a half to safety. Neither of us knew how far to believe the other. He stoked his boiler some more, and I gulped down the CC and water, trying to pass the stinking liquid over my tastebuds and into my throat, where it was warm and cool at the same time. I told Booker about the black ice on the pond in winter, and he replied that we ought to go roller skating next time.

We caught a cab to my house. It would be a long, expensive ride, but it was clear that there was no other way to get me back to Yeadon by twelve. It was also becoming clear that

Booker's boiler was boiling over. He had been fine at the bar. He had walked out and hailed a cab. Then, he leaned on me heavily to get in and slumped on the seat. His speech slurred in the middle of a sentence. "Oh, Christ," he said, "it's hitting me."

It was indeed as if he had been hit. One minute he was walking and talking, and the next he was like a fighter who'd been slugged. We'd been told at school about the dangers of ingesting too much alcohol too fast. My friends told stories about students who had died in fraternity drinking bouts, suicidal show-off rounds that left strapping young men stone dead.

"You all right?" the driver asked.

"Fine." Booker wheezed the word. "I need a smoke," he told me.

I lit a cigarette and gave it to him. I watched each time he brought it, with excruciating concentration, to his lips to make sure that he did not burn himself or me. He opened the window to get some air and panted at the breeze like a sick dog on his last ride to the veterinarian's. The taxi sped through the night toward Yeadon. We neared the graveyard where the word FERNWOOD grew in ragged topiary on a green hill. The taxi stopped at the light just before a narrow bridge over Cobbs Creek.

"I'ma be sick," Booker said.

The light turned green. The taxi began to move.

"Wait! Stop!" I called to the driver. I reached across to help Booker unlatch the door. He leaned over, and I held onto his waist with all my strength. Booker was reed thin, but six feet tall is six feet tall, and gravity was pulling him toward the ground. He vomited onto the street, for what seemed a long time.

"You all right? He all right?" the driver asked.

What could I answer?

"All right," Booker bawled it out. He flung his upper body upright, back into the taxi, and slammed the door.

"I can't believe it," he said to me.

The taxi lurched forward, laboring up the hill past the cemetery. The cicadas sent up waves of racket, their curious dry sound borne along the moist, grass-scented summer air that blew in the windows.

"Call myself taking the girl out for a good time and end up puking on the street like a bum," Booker said. "Ain't that a bitch?" Then he dozed.

"You want to take him home first?" the driver asked me.

"No." Booker revived. "No. We take the lady home first. Said I'd get you home by midnight. I'ma get you home by midnight."

I directed the driver to my house. Booker, who had seemed himself again, could not move his long legs to let me out. I climbed over him and felt him grabbing at my hands.

"What?" My sympathy for him threatened to evaporate in a moment. If he touched me, I thought, I'd slug him.

"Here. Will you wait a minute? Please! Here." He was trying to hand me a wad of money. He waved toward the driver. "Pay him."

I exhaled relief. "How much is the fare?" I asked the driver.

He did not tell me. Instead, he began to shout that he needed to know he was going to get paid for the whole trip, the whole trip. "Where the hell am I going? I got to get paid."

"You will get paid," I said to him. I spoke clearly and precisely, conscious, as the smell of vomit wafted sweet and sour off Booker's breath through the open window, of the confident speech St. Paul's had given me. I asked the driver to estimate the fare back to Booker's address. Then I rounded up his liberal guess and gave him a ten-dollar tip as well.

"Thank you for your patience," I said as if his job were finished.

"How'm I going to get him out of the car?"

"He'll get out of the car," I said as if I knew what I was talking about. I tried to give Booker the rest of his money. I was holding a bunch of wadded-up twenties.

"Keep it. You keep it," he said. "You deserve it."

I heard my mother, who was still awake, calling me from the front door. I told Booker good-night and told the taxi driver to roll. Then I walked up the front path, past the yew bushes, to the porch.

"Where's your date?" My mother asked this as we two watched the taxi cab make his U-turn and speed away. "Don't young men walk girls to the door anymore?"

"Well, Mama, we saw you at the front door, so we knew I was safe," I joked, trying to hold in my CC-and-water breath until she turned to go in.

"You're lucky your father's not home yet," she said. " 'Cause you are late, and you know he's not crazy about that boy or old man or whatever he is."

I tiptoed up the stairs in order not to wake my sister. I went directly to bed with the excuse that I had to work the seven-to-eleven shift the next day.

"Seems like you should have thought of that earlier." The dog came into my room and settled on the bed with a disgruntled sigh. It took a long time for me to go to sleep.

I awoke late, rushed to wake my father, and drove too fast to the diner. Daddy rapped on the dashboard with his knuckles to tell me to slow down. We knocked our way to work. Booker was there when I arrived.

I poured a cup of coffee and a glass of grapefruit juice as I always did, and went right to work. The day manager raised his eyebrows at me, and the waitress who had covered for me for fifteen minutes made a great show of handing over the checks on the tables she had served. Later, when I had a minute free, I went behind the steam tables and handed Booker the rest of his money, sixty or seventy dollars. He looked at it with bloodshot eyes. "You know you didn't have to give this back to me," he said. "I didn't even remember."

"It's your money," I said.

He said that I had class, even if I was just a kid, and that the next time he was going to take me out to some class spots, but he never did. We acted as if our schedules wouldn't jibe, but the truth was that we'd both seen enough. When the summer was gone, we said that we'd missed our chance until Christmas break.

By then I had saved money and taken my driving test in my mother's old station wagon. My parents trusted me to drive alone with my sister. I took her on outings to fast-food restaurants and playgrounds. I played at being the older sister I had always wanted. Carole rewarded me by copying my movements, my inflections, my idioms. I combed her hair— gently, because she was tenderheaded, as we said. I drew pictures with her and played dress-up with our mother's party gowns. They smelled of closet dust when we pulled them over our heads.

We walked to the playground behind the swim club we never joined. It was called The Nile, and had been built by the black doctors and lawyers and teachers on Yeadon's west end after they had been barred from the Yeadon Swim Club on the other side of the borough. We listened to the music and smelled the French fries. The water sounded cool, and the children were noisy. I do not remember wanting to go into the swim club; it was yet another social world to figure out and fit into, and did not seem worth the effort.

Carole and I sat on the swings that once excited her but were now too tame. We climbed into the V in the middle of the old weeping willow tree and talked about when we were smaller and when we'd grow up. She never tired of hearing anecdotes from her own childhood, and she particularly liked to hear how feisty she had been, how she had walked around the backyard naked, how she had run away to Mrs. Evans's house, how she created her own pantry of stolen cookies and candy in her room and was not discovered until an army of ants marched in a line over the windowsill, across the room, under her bed, and gave her away. She still had that same throaty, infectious laugh, but she seemed to laugh less frequently now.

Once, when I was baby-sitting for Carole and two of her friends, a sister and a brother who lived two doors away, Carole argued with the little girl and hit her. I scolded Carole while the child cried and the younger boy looked on. When I went into the house to fix their lunch, Carole hit her again. I scooped Carole under my arm and carried her upstairs. She shouted and screamed, and I felt a terrible rage erupting within me. It was hot that day. I never knew what to do when the children fought, and that summer they were fighting all the time. It was much worse with me than with the mothers. I was losing control.

"I hate you," she screamed. I slapped her. Knowing full well what I was doing, I slapped her. I knew how hurt she would be, and I did it anyway. She stopped crying immediately and stared at me, disbelieving. I had never done that to her before, and in that moment, our entire relationship was redefined. I had become one of the grown-ups (and with that most immature of actions, a blow). I might play at sibling solidarity, but now she and I knew that I had become capable of grown-up treachery.

I was one of the women, now, as I had been when I'd stood in front of the mirror in Simpson the night that Ricky had come to St. Paul's, my eyes wild and hair stuck up like a marmoset's on the top of my head. It did not come, this woman-hood, as I had expected. I had thought it was power that they had been keeping all to themselves, and it was, of a sort: power to make Ricky cry, or to strike shame into a child and wipe away, with the back of my hand, the delicate teardrops of her trust.

After the moment of shocked silence between us, I grabbed Carole to me and held her. I told her that I was sorry for hitting her, so sorry for hitting her. I asked her to behave with Roslyn, to please, please behave, and she knew and I knew that I was begging her because I no more had the ability to tolerate failing in her than in myself. She went downstairs and outside to friends who were waiting to see what had happened to her. I sat in her room for a moment letting the image of her face burn into me. I can see it even now: that dumbfounded shock, not disputing, but hating, grieving, and so quickly accepting my right to hurt her.

Later in the summer, my mother's clan—my Nana Hamil-ton, my paralyzed Aunt Emily, my octogenarian great-grandfather, and my Aunt Evelyn—moved to a tract house in suburban Wilmington. We went down in a caravan of cars, and I watched as the white neighbors came out to help our disabled kin into the house. I thought of Carole and me then, as I watched them going into the new house, the last of my family to leave the black inner city where I grew up. My great-grandfather said a prayer to bless the house, and I listened as my folks told the new neighbors what family people we were. My grandmother spread her arms and said, as she had said before, that she loved her girls ferociously.

I had always squirmed under the word and how she belted it out vaudeville-style, rolling the r, and tossing her head. I thought I knew why it had disturbed me, now that I had struck my sister and seen the panicked acceptance in her beautiful coffee-colored eyes. I knew our ferocious love better now: It was feline, deliberate, personal. Nana loved us as a lioness loved her cubs, insisting that her pride stay near and hunt with her, eat with her. Males who could not live with the pride were cast out. I also suspected that like a lioness giving birth, she would lick us, not just to clean us, or to augment her own strength, but also to discover our defects, and, if need be, if one were too weak, to swallow us up.

By the end of August, after my summer holiday in the real world, I was more than ready to go back to school.

Chapter Ten

On the first day of my Sixth-Form year, I greeted new parents and studied at the Rectory. I called across the green to old friends. I told tired-looking parents how to get to their children's new houses. I helped new girls carry boxes up the stairs. I stood outside the Old Chapel to watch the new students go in for their First-Night Service. I saw their nervousness and arrogance, and I remembered my own.

The rituals this year were familiar. They included and sustained me and helped me to know where I was, to know the season, and to ease the pain of leaving the parents and family whom I looked at with new, different, critical, nostalgic eyes. I knew as precisely as a soldier where I belonged in this community, and I had the privileges and responsibilities to show me.

I also had a history here. I had been thrown off the boat docks into the icy pond. I had lived in a house, studied in the library, run on the fields, rowed on the pond, eaten in the dining rooms, prayed and sung in the Chapel. I knew the rhythm of the year, the first days of orientation and welcome, the beginning of term, term-time proper, and then the Cricket Holiday break, Parents' Day, and on and on. I had experienced failure and success.

I stopped on the paths to talk with new students, particularly new black and Hispanic students, just as Mike Russell and Lee and Maldonado and Wally had stopped to welcome me. I saw their skepticism, and I saw reflected in their eyes the poise and confidence they saw in me. After a brief talk, I'd mount my bicycle—another Sixth-Form privilege—and ride away.

Alma and I explored North Upper and settled into our new room. Like the rest of the Upper, the room was trimmed in old wood. It had two large windows that looked southwest onto long-needle pine trees. Instead of a closet, an armoire was provided for each of us, as well as the standard bed, desk, and bureau. Instead of linoleum floors like Simpson and concrete-block walls like Middle, we had pine floors and plaster walls.

In addition, our hallway was a dead end, separated from the rest of the house by a fire door. Although the door was customarily propped open, in contravention of city fire codes, we did have the option of closing it if the noise wafted up to the second floor from the stairwell (and, as Sixth Formers, we had the clout to keep it closed). We were not troubled by passersby, and we were just across the hall from the toilets and showers. Also, positioned as we were over the kitchen, we were on the main steam line. Our radiators, we learned on the first cold night, clanged and banged as if Marley's ghost were trapped inside, but they worked. They sizzled and hissed and spat drops of boiling water on our beds, and gave more heat than I'd ever dared hoped for in Simpson. So, too, did the radiators in our bathroom.

Alma liked to keep the room much warmer than I did. It was a running joke between us, but I looked forward to coming into our toasty room, where the color of the several mix-and-match woods glowed in the afternoon sun. Not only did Alma like the room warm, she liked to sit half dressed at night as we braided our hair together and talked about the day. My side of the room bristled with order. Hers was less insistently tidy.

"How come you got to start making the bed the minute your

feet hit the floor? You need to lighten up, girl. Live a little!"
Then she'd laugh, delighted with herself and at my inability to
be angry with her.

I found her lightheartedness incredible. I kept waiting, without knowing it, for some event to shake her. She accepted
rather than fought against her limitations, and she enjoyed her
strengths. When we choreographed dances together for dance
class, we learned to respect each other's bodies, and we mar-
veled, with the sharp, quick joy of adolescent insight, that our
dispositions were reflected in our movements. She was short,
fast, and playfully athletic; I was bigger, tense, controlled. We
jumped and cavorted on the dusty green carpet in our hallway,
and the old wooden floorboards underneath groaned with our
efforts.

Underneath this new, surprising friendship ran the less-than-
lovely fact, as Alma told me years later, that I had "made a
project" of her. Just as I had corrected her pitch in choir rehearsals the year before (we'd sat next to each other in the
soprano section), I now fixed her collars, coached her on a
proper point in dance, instructed her on how not to stack our
albums without first putting them back into the sleeves and
album covers.

"I *can't* study anymore. Don't you understand? My brain is
tired, and yours is, too, 'cept for you're too crazy to know it,"
she'd say at night while I prepared to begin a midnight study
session.

"Hey, did I ask you whether you were going to study?" I
asked disingenuously. "No. All I asked was if it was OK for
me to keep the lights on or if I should go somewhere else."

"Where else are you going to go?"

"I could get late sign-out to the Schoolhouse."

"Aw, come on. It's raining too hard, and you know it. I just
guess I'll read some more of this old French. Now're you happy?

I'll be looking as baggy-eyed as you tomorrow. But I guess that's the price of rooming with the vice-president of the school. You gotta uphold the standards."

Most of my friends joked about my position on Student Council, but accepted it, as Alma did. A few, I found, were not comfortable with it, or with me as I took on the mantle.

One fall evening—when the leaves had turned red and gold, and frosts came at night to knock out the mosquitoes but retreated in the daylight—I happened upon Janie and some of her friends, a circle of them sitting cross-legged on the ground. They invited me to join them and showed me a bottle of rosé that someone had secured. I was looking down on their white legs shining in the twilight. We seniors felt relaxed for the first part of the term, knowing we'd soon be grinding like maniacs, filling out college applications, writing essays, taking the standardized tests for the last time. I wanted to bask with them in the early days of Sixth-Form year. (We were already referring to ourselves with premature nostalgia.)

But I was scheduled to sit on a Disciplinary Committee meeting soon. I'd received notification in my mailbox. More and more frequently that fall, I received official notes in my box. They listed several names across the top, faculty members first, then two or three students. My name would be circled. I knew that the Rector's secretary typed these notes and photocopied them, and that each person named would receive one. I was notified of meetings, dinners for visitors, planning sessions for school functions. I attended meetings in the Schoolhouse, in Vice-Rectors' offices, and in the welcoming living room of the Student-Council adviser, a gracious French teacher named Mr. Archer. I ate lunches and dinners at Scudder, where I met again with the diminutive housekeeper who had made breakfast for my parents and me when I'd come for my interview nearly two years before. I carried plates out to her. I talked to her in order to escape for a while the repetitive discussions about school life.

Mostly, however, I took part. I learned with what care the faculty scheduled our lives, and to what degree they considered the good of the students. The Lower School was being phased out; what could we do to keep the younger boys from feeling left out of activities geared toward older teenagers? The trustees were coming. How could we arrange for more students to interact with them—not just the straight-arrows hand-picked by the administrators? Older students were allowed to take long weekends away from school, but only the wealthy or those who lived nearby could make use of the privilege. How could we give scholarship kids and students from far away a chance for a break, too? (Answer: a Student Council initiative called Long Weekend on Campus, which excused a student from Saturday classes.)

The Disciplinary Committee had not yet met that year, but we were due to convene soon. Peter Starr and I, and a group of faculty members, would hear the case of a student who had been caught breaking an "expectation" (they weren't called rules) of the school. We would deliberate and suggest a response to the Rector.

I looked around at the cross-legged kids on the grass. What I had been doing was different from what they had been doing that fall. It had not seemed so different at first, but my thinking had changed. I tried to tell Janie that I couldn't drink this year. "It just wouldn't be right," I said. "I'd like to, but I shouldn't."

"I can't believe that you've let this vice-president crap go to your head."

The others were quiet. They were watching. This was between Janie and me. It was the sort of dispute that rarely took place in company. They watched with avid interest.

"It's not going to my head," I said. "It's just that I can't sit in judgment on somebody tomorrow night knowing that I've done exactly the same thing the night before. I can't do that."

"Next thing you'll be turning us in."

According to the Honor Code, that's what I was supposed to do. I did not think it would help my case to point out that at the present moment, I was being lenient.

"I really didn't think you'd take it this way," said Janie.

"Neither did I." I had not expected that anything would change. I could lose my outrageous friend. I did not want to lose her irreverence and swagger and fun, her loyalty or brassy sexuality. I felt important with Janie, as if we knew more than others, saw more, felt more, perceived some quality through a sixth sense of headiness that others did not possess. I didn't want her to think I'd joined the establishment, but the truth was that, in a way, I had.

I went back to my hot little den to lick my wounds and convince myself, in the glow of Alma's company, that I'd found something better. And I did indeed begin to receive other, subtle rewards of my new (relatively) law-abiding status. Although I did not realize it at the time, my relations with my teachers were changing. I had little to hide from them, a state which I understood only in terms of their treatment of me: they'd stopped watching me so hard. My St. Paul's career suddenly seemed shorter. Like a fifty-year-old manager, I saw that I'd gone as far as I could go in the company, and I felt released, just a little, from the tyranny of competition.

Anthony Wade, who had teased me relentlessly the year before, noticed the change in me, and felt it incumbent upon him to tell me about it. He made me laugh. I was astonished by this new friendship, which was clearly headed toward romance. I wondered if I could date Anthony and still remain myself. He did not seem to demand that I affect a girlie witlessness. He accepted me, committee meetings and all, and he showed compassion toward my difficulty in math and my more successful struggles in science.

"Anybody who could get an HH out of Buxton's class can memorize the Periodic Table," he'd say as we walked together from the science building. "The only problem with chemistry is you can't wing it. You can't go in, read the first and last line and come out with, 'Mr. Hawley, this chemical reaction really acts as a metaphor for human relations with God as expressed in the Trinity. . . .' "

I'd make some retort, but I took his point. There was a difference in the disciplines. I'd learned that in last year's desperate battle with calculus and the more successful campaign I'd mounted in Spanish under Sr. Fuster's loving tutelage. In the fall term I was taking dance, Modern Novels, Spanish, Biology II, and chemistry. I knew that I could not afford to skitter over the basics in science. I did not know them. I would not be able to pick them up later.

These simple facts were easier to accept as I spent more time with Anthony. We studied together, met between classes, sat together at lunch. I could see up close that he, too, did the groundwork for his sciences. I could see the repetition and exercise, and I learned to believe in it.

Parents' Day turned out to be an unsettling time. My parents and my grandparents Jackson were scheduled to come to school, but at the last minute, my mother, on the recommendation of her doctor, decided to stay home. She was ill.

I was deeply disturbed by her absence. I was one of four students chosen to speak at the Parents' Day Symposium. She was not there to hear me. She had been in every audience for every skit I had performed since second grade. I was only half of the performance. She was the other.

Mr. Oates introduced me as "the first girl to be elected an officer of the School." The audience registered a suitably quiet Episcopalian appreciation. Mom would have drunk it in, but she missed it. Then Mr. Oates said that I was on the editorial board of the *Horae,* the school literary magazine. I gulped. That was wrong! I had submitted several celebration-of-blackness poems, but the *Horae* honchos had rejected them all. He said more, and I held my breath through the applause.

I stepped to the lectern and adjusted the microphone. My grandfather turned around to the people behind him. No doubt he was identifying me as his granddaughter. It made me smile, and I used the smile to slide into my speech. The moment I heard my own voice bounce back at me through the speakers, I saw someone else. It was Ethel Kennedy. I knew that her son was at St. Paul's, but a smart-mouthed Fourth Former was not the same as a famous mother. Not three sentences into the speech about diversity in the morning chapel services, my bladder leaked.

I could feel the warm betrayal like a five-year-old awakening from a dream. Pop-Pop was smiling broadly, my grandmother more discreetly; my father looked proud. I could not stand in front of these white people and wet myself! I crossed my legs behind the lectern and pulled all of myself up into my voice. I heard it deepen in the speakers. It was calm and poised. My voice finished its speech, and the rest of me sat down.

I had also prepared a special dance for my mother at the evening recital. I saw the white faces again, blurred now and small above the footlights. I smelled the heat of the footlights. The music I had chosen was repetitive and romantic. It was Dvořák's Slavonic Dance No. 2 in E minor, the kind of thing my mother loved. The melody rose up around itself, and I whirled as I had for Alma in practice after practice on the green-carpeted hall outside our room, on the thick, shiny surface of the gymnasium floor, and finally, on the Mem Hall stage. It was Mama's story: the yearning, twirling and twirling out of control, the love dance danced alone. The movements and the music were big, melodramatic, romantic. I felt foolish doing them without her there, clearing her throat in the audience.

I lost my place. There was a twirl and a drop to the floor, a roll during the quiet section, and another roll, one leg whipping around in a circle and pulling the other leg and my body with it to a sudden stop, then a pull up from face down to hands and knees, and then up to knees. Suddenly the music was ahead of me, and I knew that I should have been on my feet by then. I was on my hands and knees like a dog when I should have been leaping in the air—one, two, three leaps in the air in a tight circle, the energy closing in a tense, bent arabesque. I threw my arms up and whipped them around to pull myself upright and went right into the arabesque, but I was off by then. I had a minute more to go, and my mind was flashing mechanically through the movements. That was wrong, too, terribly wrong. I shouldn't have been thinking steps then, as if this were the second week of rehearsal. I should have known them, as I had known them two days before, when Mama said that she thought she'd be able to make it, if she drove with a pillow propped behind her bad back, and if they made several stops along the way so she would not tighten up. I knew I had to stop concentrating on the movements. I had to fix my face, and maybe the face, the right face, would discipline my mind and body.

It helped. I fixed my face, and I absorbed the attitude into me. But I had to do more if I was to go on and finish the thing. I had to fix my mind on something else—some*one* else. I thought of Anthony. He had visited one of our practices and stood in the back of the hall. I had not seen him until we were finished. He had come round to the back door outside the changing room to meet me, and he said that he liked to see me dance. We had both been shy after that, and the shyness, the privacy of the dance, was what I had missed. Once again the dance became a communion with another person. I could feel the desire of a girl alone in a forest clearing, brimming over with feelings she dared not express. That was what I had wanted to give to my mother, some dramatic token of love—and of a new inexpressible privacy on which I felt my life depended, and which I dared not reveal, so that it had become ashamed of itself and vengeful.

I accepted my family's praise with my head down. I insisted, despite their pride, on telling them what had gone wrong.

"Why, honey," my Nana said, "I couldn't see that anything went wrong at all. We thought it was just fine. Just lovely."

"That was great," Pop said, beaming.

"He told everybody that you were his granddaughter," my sister said, giggling mischievously as she ratted on him.

"Well, sure I did. Why not? She is my granddaughter, isn't she? I've got two beautiful granddaughters. Pshaw! I'm not ashamed of that!"

"Oh, Earle," my grandmother said as Pop's voice mounted with pride.

"Wha'? Should I be ashamed of that?"

We laughed. It was a standard family conversation. Pop-Pop was a man who had worn each and every tie I had ever given him. He'd wear them for years until my grandmother pointed out that they were frayed.

My father told me I'd done beautifully and put his arm around me. I felt as if I were hiding deep inside my skin, as if a whole galaxy had been set in motion inside me, and I was way out in its farthest reaches. It seemed a long way from my insides to the surface of my shoulders, where Daddy's arm rested, or my fingers, where my sister's small hand held tight.

After Parents' Day, when I received a letter from Ricky asking why I had not written in four months, I finally wrote back that I was through. I vowed when I dropped the letter into the box that I'd never let myself get trapped again. I tried to congratulate myself on my new maturity and assertion, but I had to admit that had Anthony and I not gotten together, I would have dodged even longer. The correspondence coughed out a few more letters, and then was still. But the relationship, on my end, lived like a haunt in my soul, reminding me, whenever I was inclined to forget, to trust no man.

By early November, many of our formmates had decided which colleges they would apply to. A few were submitting early-decision applications. I didn't like to think about college. The fact was that Stanford University had captured my imagination (in part because I confused it with Berkeley, which I'd further confused with San Francisco State, where the first department of Afro-American studies was established).

In my presence, Mr. Quirk, our college adviser, called the Stanford admissions officer. They were willing to pay for me to fly to California for an interview and to visit the university.

"I can't go," I told him. My mother's health remained "dicey," as she said. It was bad enough that I had left Philadelphia for New Hampshire, but how could I even think of going across the country?

"There's no harm in taking a look at the place," Mr. Quirk said. "You can go on out there, get a feel for it, and then decide. Listen, your mother's health may improve by next year this time. Don't close the door."

I did not trust myself. Already I wanted to blast out of responsibility and go to a place so far away that I could afford only one trip home a year. I had to stop myself (and Mr. Quirk). I could not take the trip, I said, knowing that I did not intend to go. It would be like stealing from the scholarship fund. Now that I'd made the moral argument, I couldn't retrench. I'd stay on the East Coast.

I thought of applying to Radcliffe, but I didn't like Cambridge. Finally I settled on two universities near home. One was Princeton, because F. Scott Fitzgerald, the writer who articulated my fearful suspicions about my white schoolmates, had gone there. The University of Pennsylvania, in Philadelphia, was the other. Since I was a toddler, I'd seen the ivy-covered brick walls and the great iron gates of Penn through the windows of the Number 40 bus on the way to my grandmother's office. Only Penn students could go in. I applied, no doubt, to see inside the courtyard.

My mother's illness worsened. I went more frequently than usual to the phone booth behind the Upper to call home, only to receive more insistent denial. Neither my mother nor father told me precisely what was wrong. Instead, they assured me that Mom was being taken care of, that she had the best care available, that she seemed to be responding to treatment. "You just keep doing the best you can up there," my mother told me in a weak voice. "That's how you can help me get well."

My worry grew into fury at being coddled and shut out. I called one afternoon, early enough so that I knew that my sister would be home from school but my father would not yet have returned from work. Sure enough, Carole answered the phone. My mother was in bed, she told me, and she'd been in bed. It didn't seem to Carole that Mom was getting better, although she, too, she said, received daily reassurances.

Once again, as on Parents' Day, I felt the disturbance. I reacted crazily, physically, dumbly, like rats to a change in the atmosphere before a hurricane. The feeling continued. It tensed and worsened like my mother's back. And the news grew more confusing. The back problem, it seemed, might actually be caused by a tumor growing on another organ but pressing on her spine. How could I stay at school, twiddling around at meetings about long weekends, when my mother was bedridden? The worst of it was that no one had forced me to go to St. Paul's. She hadn't made me. I had left her. I had done this to myself.

I missed Chapel. I skipped classes and failed to hand in homework. I had no excuses, except to apologize. Pink slips for Saturday-night detention appeared in my mailbox. I do not remember how I reacted. I cannot even recall what I was doing while I cut my commitments. I was numb with frozen rage. It was all I could do to mark time and keep up a front.

After just a few days, I received a note in my box summoning me to the Rector's office. The note was typed, not photocopied, and it did not mention an agenda.

Mr. Oates greeted me with a tight, quick smile. It was the barest of his welcomes, but it was a welcome nonetheless. He motioned me to sit down in a chair in front of his polished desk. To my left the afternoon light and the autumn air tumbled in through the open casement windows. From his windows he had a view of the green in front of the Schoolhouse. It was bounded on one side by a newish, red-brick dormitory house and on the other by Christian Row, three rambling clapboard houses for masters. The green was bisected by the main road through the grounds. On the other side was the Chapel, where St. Paul stood in bronze, his finger pointed in the air, his robes in midflap, zealous and evangelical. It was difficult not to look out the windows—they made a pretty little bay, and there was a window seat under them—particularly while Mr. Oates's blue-gray eyes were the alternative. They bore down on me. I had tried to convince myself that this meeting might have to do with general school business. It didn't. This was personal.

"Libby, I'll come right to the point. You've missed several commitments in the past few days."

I felt myself grow stiff with defiance. Mr. Oates said that I had responsibilities, particularly now that I was a school officer. He did not generally call students in for a personal talk after a few missed commitments, he continued, but he wanted me to know, and know early, before I'd gone any further, that this was serious and that he was concerned to tell me that he himself, the Rector, cared about me. He cared that there might be underlying this behavior some change of attitude, some problem. He wanted to get at the problem, he said, before the behavior, which could jeopardize my position, my good relations, my college prospects, got any worse.

I took the last as a threat. The old nun from the movie came back to me, giving me an inappropriate urge to laugh out loud: "I have read the word of our Lord God until my eyes burned like the very fires of hell. . . ."

What did they know about me? About how it felt to be trapped in a world of wealth? What did he know about being trotted out for visitors who spoke to me as a sociological curiosity?

I suspected that I was being treated like a volatile compound. The last black school officer, after all, had been deposed for plagiarism. No doubt the entire unseemly spectacle of my falling apart the previous spring was common knowledge: the calculus debacle, my crash at the infirmary, dropping crew, signing up for five arts courses this year, only to reverse myself after a letter from the Vice-Rector. I was indeed unstable, raw, exposed. Mr. Oates was talking to me slowly and firmly, as one does to a child who is not listening or an old person who cannot hear.

"My mother is sick!" I blurted it out. How could classes and Chapel seem important when my family was in trouble, my mother sick, and, although I did not say it, my parents barely speaking to each other? I did not want to cry there in the Rector's presence, except that he said so sincerely that he was sorry, and he said that it was well nigh impossible to concentrate for anyone, adults, too, when someone one loved was in pain.

The Schoolhouse hallways were quiet in the afternoon. The secretaries made businesslike sounds outside the Rector's door: typewriters clacked; telephones rang; and the women spoke in hushed, sibilant voices. Inside his office the sun glowed orange off the wood panels. I wanted to rest, and this office was restful. The power in it guaranteed that we would not be interrupted, which could not be said of many other places on the grounds.

"Why haven't you taken a long weekend? I'm sure your teachers would be more than happy to excuse you to go home to see your mother."

It was always so simple for people here, I thought. So simple. Just take care of things, that's what they did, and then wondered why the rest of the world was in such a funk. "I don't have the money to fly home." It galled me to say so.

"I see," he said.

I left rigid with self-righteous anger to look for Jimmy.

Jimmy was not in any of the usual places, so I walked in the woods and sat on the docks for a while. When I came back onto the main green, I stopped at the post office out of habit; it was what we all did each time we passed. In my box was another small St. Paul's envelope. I assumed it was a meeting notice. I opened it to find another letter from the Rector. He had arranged permission for my weekend, and I was to see Mr. Price about plane tickets and money for incidental traveling expenses.

Mr. Price, too, had been busy, while I had raged through

the woods. "Take the bus to Boston," he said when I got to his apartment, "and please, please, take a cab to the airport. St. Paul's School can afford it."

Mr. Price could not help saying that he wished I had told him earlier that I was worried. "We could have arranged this a lot sooner. That's what I'm here for."

I wanted to reassure him, but I could see in my mind's eye the image of him as he stood outside the post office the year before with a jewelry box in his hand. He had brought a pair of earrings as a gift for Carmen, who was one of his favorites, and as she squealed with delight and reached to take the box, he had pulled it back behind his back. "Don't be too greedy," he had teased.

I remembered the course I had taken with him the winter before, Black and White Survey, and how ashamed I was that he came to class clearly bored or unprepared. "Any comments, questions?" I could not pretend to trust him, and yet, he had made arrangements on my behalf.

"Thank you for what you've done," I said. "And also for all the things we take for granted. I'm thinking of your driving us to Cambridge each week." (Along with half a dozen other students I was taking an evening course at Harvard. It was an African-history lecture where the professor spun wild tales about Chaka Zulu, the warrior who impaled his enemies on sharpened stakes in the ground.) I welcomed an honest rush of gratitude to the man who had first introduced me to the school, but in whom I no longer had confidence.

I did not call my mother at the hospital until I arrived at our house. I seem to remember that no one else was home. It was about half past seven; visiting hours ended at eight. I drove my mother's station wagon fast to the hospital. The back end fish-tailed as I swung around corners through Fairmount Park.

When I got to my mother's floor, the nurses told me that visiting hours were over for the night.

"I've just come straight from New Hampshire," I said breathlessly.

The nurses looked stern, but they let me into her room. My mother had combed her hair and put on her bathrobe for me.

"I saw you drive up," she said. "And I saw you flicking my car around with one arm hanging out the window. Didn't I tell you to use two hands while you're driving?"

"Uh-huh." I began to laugh.

"And when you leave here, I want you to use two hands on the wheel."

"Uh-huh," I said, still laughing.

"You're going to do whatever the hell you want, aren't you?"

"Uh-huh."

She made a pout. "Hard head makes soft behind. Didn't I tell you to stay at school? So now you see me. Are you satisfied?"

I was satisfied that I had done something, but my mother did not look good. She was worried and fearful. She looked as if she had been hit and was waiting to be hit again, or as if she were trapped. It made her face into a mask that only laughter dispelled, and that just for a moment.

The next morning I visited her again. I told her about the dance I'd performed on Parents' Weekend and how it wasn't right without her.

Mom told me that her back pain was being caused by "female trouble" and referred vaguely to tests. I left Philadelphia not knowing how bad off she was, if or when she'd get better, or how. For what purpose, I wanted to know, did she keep information from me? Five years before, I had run to show her the blood in my underwear, and she'd laughed.

("But why didn't you tell me?"

"You didn't need to know.")

It didn't occur to me that I never named my own mystery illness the spring before (except to misdiagnose it to friends as mono), because I'd been afraid to admit, even to my mother, how much I'd wanted to lie down somewhere and hide. Black women, tall and strong as cypress trees, didn't pull that. Pain and shame and cowardice and fear had to be kept secret. A great-aunt moved to Boston and passed for white. My mother's father, once he remarried, pastored a church and never talked about his three daughters. My father's father, who'd been divorced away years before, was mentioned seldom, in a whisper; I never saw him, never saw his photo. My mother and father went for weeks barely speaking to each other. And I never told what happened that night with Ricky in the dark. Trust no man.

I walked through secrets that were like an animate forest with watchful shadows. It never occurred to me that I kept them myself, or that what I liked most about sitting on the Disciplinary Committee was the chance to penetrate other people's.

We started each D.C. by reading the student's written statement of wrongdoing. Our job was not to determine guilt like a jury, but to try to understand what had happened and why, and to recommend disciplinary action to the Rector.

After Peter and I and the three teachers on the committee had read the statement, the student and his faculty and student advocates spoke. They talked about the incident, but also about the pattern of the student's development at school. Advocates generally argued that the rule-breaking was the final symptom of some general crisis—which had now passed. Groupmasters were often the most hard-nosed advocates. After the statements, committee members asked questions. Sometimes they were painful. They wanted to know about the students' relationships at school and at home. We were alert to news of change: divorces, sibling trouble, breaking up with steadys, hints of drug or alcohol abuse.

I learned to think of misbehavior as symptom rather than disease. A girl who was caught with a boy in her room might be an indiscreet friend or girlfriend. She might be testing the rules. She might just have been self-absorbed, as we all were so many times, wanting a private place to console a friend after a family death. But she might also have created a string of disturbances in the house, escalating in importance. In that case the committee argued, after the defendant and company had left the room, in hopes of finding responses that would not just punish, but teach the wrongdoer—and the rest of us.

This was new-style discipline to me. I didn't know if I approved, but I looked forward to each session. I saw big, tough boys' eyes fill with tears when they realized how they'd jeopardized their place at school—or betrayed a friend. I listened as perfectly put-together girls lied to us, and walked out certain that they'd pulled it off. I looked forward to the inexplicable feeling of forgiveness that came over me at the end of a session. That, too, was a secret.

Chapter Eleven

During the winter term Bruce Chan, who had drafted me to look after Fumiko on the first day of my Fifth Form, suggested that we begin tutoring some of the younger students in English. He also delegated me to write a letter of protest to the English department for what we thought was prejudice against the incoming students of color. (One teacher, by way of correcting a young student's paper, commented on the pattern of grammatical errors and warned the boy that he'd have to work to overcome his black English. We suspected, after reading several papers, that our teachers judged typically black "errors" more harshly than others, and that once obsessed by idiom they lost sight of black students' ideas.) A few days later I gritted my teeth as Bruce edited my letter in red pen. I remember delivering the rewritten version to the department chairman, who responded that he and the other teachers worked hard to be as sensitive as possible to the needs of all the students, but that he would urge his teachers, as he had been doing, to even greater consideration.

The tutoring was equally frustrating. Students brought us their papers during free periods before class. They wanted us to tidy things up, plug in big words. They did not come with a rough draft, as we asked, prepared to rethink and rewrite.

The best I could do, I decided, was to try to build their

confidence rather than tear it down. I tried to pick out their original ideas and show them that these, the scary ones, were worth writing about.

"Forget your notes; put them away until exams. The papers are yours. It's how *you* read the same old story that that man has been teaching for twenty years. He's waiting for *you* to see it fresh. And you *can*. You've brought a whole bunch of new ideas that haven't been here until now."

When the girl left, I heard my own words. I had never said them before, never even thought them. I sat in my room grinning. More than anything I had said while I stood nervously trying to solicit discussion on blues lyrics, a half-hour with that girl and her no-thesis, no-introduction, no-proper-conclusion paper had shown me that I, too, had something to give to St. Paul's. I had come not just with my hat in my hand, a poorly shod scholarship girl, but as a sojourner bearing gifts, which were mine to give or withhold.

No doubt, the appearance of Miss Clinton that year gave me strength. The new black Spanish teacher was in her early twenties. She was dark and thin with high pockets and a high bark of a laugh if you caught her in a funny mood outside of class. In class was a different matter. She would step outside the classroom, kick the doorstop with one sensible shoe, and say clearly over her shoulder: *"¡Listos, ya!"*

Her mouth with its pointed top lip was beautiful when she spoke, and the language came out bright and precise: "Ready, now!" Those of us who were not in her class stood in the sunny hallway in the modern-languages wing of the Schoolhouse on purpose to hear her. We yelped when she said it—not *ahora,* meaning now, but *¡ya!* Immediately! She was tough.

"Hell, no, they're not ready," we'd say as we walked back to the Reading Room across the hall.

"They're not *even* ready."

"They will never be ready."

"They better get ready."

"Forget it. Those guys are smoked. *Smoked!*"

The other teachers did not treat Miss Clinton with condescending politeness (as many did another young black teacher). I could not tell whether they offered her friendship, but I could see that they gave her respect.

And no mistaking she was black. Now and then Miss Clinton drove into town to buy greens—fresh greens in Concord—and she'd boil a big pot. It stunk up her tiny dormitory; it seeped into the Indian tapestries on students' walls. On Saturday evening I watched her dance to her new Marvin Gaye album, and I realized how lonely she might be, this energetic young woman, for a companion. But she neither hid it from us nor slopped it onto us to carry.

I took courage from her, as much as I dared, and yet I feared her, too. I feared judgment that never came.

"You should stop by more often," she said as I stirred her pot and moistened my face in the steam.

Buoyed up by Miss Clinton, my head crammed with the literature I was teaching under Mr. Lederer, who spent his sabbatical year teaching in a North Philadelphia high school, I began to feel more confident in the inevitable racial discussions in classes, at Seated Meal, after visitors' talks. I took the offensive and bore my gifts proudly. What the discussions concerned specifically, who was there, where they took place, I do not remember. I do recall hearing the same old Greek-centered, European-centered assumptions of superiority. Might made right. I had my stories about Chaka Zulu from my Harvard evening course (and I knew they worshipped Harvard!). Nothing mattered. I was like a child again, trying to argue that I was still somebody—I am Somebody! as we shouted back to Jesse Jackson on the television—even though black people had been slaves, even though we hadn't had the dignity to jump off the boats en masse or die from tuberculosis like the Indians. More facts. I wanted more facts to show that it wasn't all fair now, that the resources that kept them here, ruddy and well-tutored, as healthy as horses, had been grabbed up in some greedy, obscene, unfair competition years before.

"Even if my great-grandfather did own slaves, it's not fair to hold me responsible."

Fair. Fair. Fair. They shouted fair, as if fair had anything to do with it, and I had no facts to wipe their words away. I had no words for their trust funds, capital gains, patrimonies, legacies, bequests. My mind screamed profanities. I had no other words. They had taken them and made them into lies.

That's how I felt the night I left a racial discussion with a girl named India Bridgeman. A group of black girls had once asked her to take the role of plantation overseer in a student-choreographed dance. I'd kept in my head the image of her as she danced around the slaves with a whip, her classical ballet training showing in every movement. She'd visited England as a member of St. Paul's varsity field hockey team. She was an acolyte who knew the rituals of high mass: where to walk, what to carry. I knew her through Janie, but mostly I envied her from a distance as a symbol, a collection of accomplishments that I did not possess.

We continued the debate into the Upper and then up the stairs to her room. She turned toward me, and I saw India the dancer. She pivoted on the balls of her feet, calf muscles bunched, sternum up. On her forehead was a light brown spot that I had thought she penciled on as an affected beauty mark. (It was a mole.) She had clear eyes, kissy lips, and big, dramatic movements. "Wait, wait a minute! Wait, wait, wait, wait!" India talked like that.

"I get it," she said. "I get it. You know how when you *get* something that you've never been able to know before?"

I nodded, but I resisted her enthusiasm, and the spontaneous humility of this sudden expansiveness. India translated what I had been saying into different words, and I listened, dumbfounded to hear them. It was clear that she, too, knew how it felt to be an outsider. I had never suspected it. India told me about her life growing up in Manhattan, and her own estrangement from many of our schoolmates. We talked until we grew hungry.

"Isn't there anything to eat, anywhere?" India jumped up from the floor, where we'd been sitting, and walked across the room to her stash. "All I've got is mayonnaise," she said as if the world would end. "Hold everything! I know I had some crackers, too. Do you think that's gross, just putting mayonnaise on crackers?"

"Are you kidding? I was raised on mayonnaise. And mayonnaise, not that cheap-ass salad dressing." I cut my eyes to the little jar in her hand. She whooped with laughter.

"What would you have done if I'd been holding some 'cheap-ass salad dressing'?"

"I would have died. But really, that stuff—"

"I know, I know, it's awful," she agreed.

"My mother makes mayonnaise sandwiches. My whole family does. And my grandmother! God forbid she should have a few drinks. You should see what she does. *That's* awful."

I had not talked to other girls at St. Paul's about my grandmother. India laughed with me, but solicitously, watchfully, as if to judge how much I could take, or how far beneath the surface of humor lay the shame.

"My *other* grandmother," I said, having risked as much as I dared just then, "sends me care packages, and I think I have some juice. Do you like pear nectar?"

"Not really."

"I used to love it. I don't have the heart to tell her I'm not so crazy about it now."

"I know. It's like they get one thing that they know makes you happy, and they'll buy it for you for the rest of your life." She stopped eating a cracker. "Oh, that's *so* dear. That's so beautiful that your grandmother does that. Do you have any more?"

"Sure. It's hot, though."

"Oh, let's get it. Let's drink to—what do you call her?"

"Nana."

"Let's drink to Nana."

We tiptoed to my room, and I pulled my pantry box out from underneath my bed. "Do you like sardines?" I whispered.

"Why not?"

India and I talked often and late into the night after that. We raged together at St. Paul's School—at its cliques and competitiveness; its ambivalence toward its new female members; its smugness and certainty and power. We talked about families and boyfriends, girls we liked and girls we didn't. We laughed at how we had appeared to each other the year before. Our talk was therapeutic, private, and as intense as romance. It was for me the first triumph of love over race.

Outside my personal circle, the school that term seemed to buzz, buzz. Class officers, it seemed, were often called upon to talk. We talked day and evening, in club activities and rehearsals, in the houses, in the hallways, in our rooms, in the bathrooms, and in meetings after meetings. We gossiped. We criticized. We whined. We analyzed. We talked trash. We talked race relations, spiritual life, male-female relations, teacher-student trust. We talked confidentially. We broke confidences and talked about the results. We talked discipline and community. We talked Watergate and social-fabric stuff.

I did not follow the Watergate hearings. I did not rush to

the third floor of the Schoolhouse for the ten-thirty *New York Times* delivery to read about it; nor did I crowd around the common-room TV to watch the proceedings. I could not bother to worry about which rich and powerful white people had hoodwinked which other rich and powerful white people. It seemed of a piece with their obsession with fairness.

I was unprepared, therefore, to dine at the Rectory with Mr. Archibald Cox, the St. Paul's alumnus whom President Nixon had fired when, as U.S. Special Prosecutor, Mr. Cox began to reveal the Watergate break-in and cover-up. Seated around him were the Rector and a handful of faculty members and student leaders. I said as little as possible in order to conceal my ignorance. Mr. Cox was acute. He referred to the Watergate players and the major events in witty shorthand. I couldn't quite follow, so I ate and smiled and made periodic conversation noises.

Then he wanted to hear about St. Paul's School. There had been so many changes since his time. I found myself saying, in answer to his question, or the Rector's signal, that I was more aware of being black at St. Paul's than I was of being a girl. I used a clever phrase that I stole from somewhere and hoped he hadn't already heard: "Actually, we're still more like . . . a boys' school with girls in it. But black people's concerns—diversifying the curriculum and that sort of thing—the truth is that that's more important to me than whether the boys have the better locker room."

Pompous it was, and I knew it, but better to be pompous in the company of educated and well-off white folk, better even to be stone wrong, than to have no opinion at all.

Mr. Cox thought a moment. God forbid he should go for the cross-examination. I added more. "Black concerns here at school may look different, but are not really, from the concerns that my parents have taught me all my life at home." I put that

one in just so he'd know that I had a family. "And believe me,
sir, my mama and daddy did not put President Nixon into the
White House. *We* didn't do that!"

Mr. Cox wrinkled his lean, Yankee face into a mischievous
smile. His voice whispered mock conspiracy. He leaned toward
me. "Do you know who Nixon hates worst of all?"

I shook my head no. I had no idea.

"Our kind of people."

My ears felt hot. I wanted to jump on the table. I wanted to
go back home and forget that I'd ever come. I wanted to take
him to West Philly, and drop him off at the corner of Fifty-
second and Locust, outside Foo-Foo's steak emporium, right
by the drug dealers, and leave him there without a map or a
bow tie. Then tell me about our kind of people.

The Rector gave me a look that urged caution. I fixed my
face. "What kind of people are those?" I asked.

"Why, the educated Northeastern establishment," he said.

The Rector smiled as if relieved.

Soon after, I received a note to meet another visitor: Mr.
Vernon Jordan, president of the National Urban League. During his talk to students, Mr. Jordan referred to incidents in the
history and current affairs of black and white racial relations
that I had never heard. I felt the relief of a child after she has
walked a very long way trying to be brave. Afterward I could
not think of one intelligent question to ask him. It felt good
simply to ride awhile. The next morning Alma and I met him
at Scudder. Mr. Jordan was finishing breakfast when we arrived. He asked us about ourselves and the school. Alma described my involvement in Student Council and teased me
about my reluctance to talk. "She's usually a big talker," she
said.

I told him about Alma's athletic achievements, her varsity
letters in basketball and lacrosse. We mentioned our Third

World Coalition, and admitted our squabbles, our struggles, how at times we felt constricted, but could not figure out what to do.

He understood us. He caught up our words and showed us what we meant. "This is a new phase of civil rights," he said. "Just a few years ago, it was a lot clearer. You could point to outrageously racist laws. Now it's more subtle. You kids here are feeling the effects. I mean you're here—" he motioned his hand in the air to take in the graceful room. We could hear Mrs. Burrows washing dishes in the kitchen. "And it's hard not to become a part of all this. It's hard not to forget where we came from."

How could I tell him: forgetting wasn't the problem, it was finding a new way to fight. If we couldn't fight, we'd implode. I tried to say that. I tried to ask him what we should do now, in this new phase. It was time for him to go to Mem Hall, but he hadn't told us how to go on. I wanted to beg, to demand that he show us the way. "The most important thing," he said, "is to get everything you can here. You kids are getting a view of white America that we never even got close to." He shook his head. "We couldn't even dream of it."

I thought of the scene in *Native Son*—I'd have to teach it soon to the Fourth Formers—where the two boys stand on the sidewalk looking at an airplane. Only white boys could fly, they said.

"You've got to get as much as you can here, be the *best* that you can, so that when you come out, you'll be ready. But you cannot forget where you've come from."

When I had been eleven years old, the year before Martin Luther King was shot, I had written to the Southern Christian Leadership Conference headquarters in Atlanta asking them what I could do to help the struggle. They had said the same thing. Stay in school. Prepare yourself. Then what?

"The fact is," he said, "there's no blueprint for what we're doing now. It's all uncharted water. We're going to need you. We're going to need every one of you."

I wolfed down Mr. Jordan's visit like every other experience at St. Paul's. I had no time to digest it. Mr. Cox came and went. Mr. Jordan came and went. Over Long Winter Weekend, we students who were staying at school slept late and lingered lazily over our meals. Valentine's Day arrived. Anthony put a card in my mailbox, and my grandmother Jackson sent me a card, with "a little paper money," as she said, tucked in. I took it to town to buy toiletries. That night, I found that Jimmy had been in town, too.

"Jimmy's looking for you," his roommate told me. "He needs to talk to you. Now."

"What is it?" Jimmy never sent messages.

"I think he should tell you."

"I got to get out of this dorm," Jimmy said when I arrived. We went to the skatehouse, but on Saturday night it was full of people. So we went to the squash courts, picked a court, and closed the door. The court was white and empty. Someone in another court was practicing. We heard the balls hit and zing off the walls. In a week, the student work squad would be assigned to wash the black strike marks.

It had begun at the supermarket in town. Jimmy had taken a carton of cigarettes and was stopped on his way out by a security guard who hustled him to the manager. The manager listened to Jimmy's apology. "I was begging her, please. I told her that I didn't know why I had done it, that I'd never do it again. I'd never come into the store again! I'm blurting all this out to her about how I was from St. Paul's School and there was all this pressure, and I must have lost my mind. I offered to do anything I could to make up for it. She must have seen what a state I was in, because she told me that she was willing to let me go without pressing charges if I could find an adult who was willing to come get me."

Jimmy asked her to call a black family he knew in town. It was characteristic of him to have found these people and made the effort to get to know them. They were not home, however, when she called. While Jimmy was sitting outside the manager's office, she telephoned the school and was referred to Jimmy's groupmaster, Mr. Price.

Mr. Price came to the store, thanked the manager, and assured her that the incident would not be repeated. When they got into the car, Jimmy said, Mr. Price slammed the door. "He started screaming and cursing at me," Jimmy told me. "He was like: 'You are screwed, Jimmy Hill.'

"It was like he had been waiting on this, like he was really going to get off on seeing me screwed. I know that's not my imagination.

"I know what I did was wrong. Hey, look, I'm willing to do anything I can to make up. I don't know what made me pick up those cigarettes! It was like, I wanted them, and I didn't have enough money, and it's a great, big store. . . ."

"You could have asked me," I moaned. "I got some money this week."

"I know that. I know. That's what makes this whole thing so stupid. I could have asked Dorien. Dorien's loaded. I could have got it off any of the white kids. They'll give you money in a minute. Why not?

"I just did it. Like, they're not going to miss this one little carton of smokes. *I know it's wrong.* I know it. I'm not trying to make excuses. But Mr. Price is out to get me. It's like no matter what the school decides, he wants me screwed. Personally. And I can't figure out why. I never did the man any harm." He smiled wanly. "You got a cigarette? Obviously, I didn't get any this afternoon."

We went outside to stand in the butt-littered snow and smoke. Jimmy asked me about the disciplinary process. It gave me chills to describe it to him. I had sat on the committee half a year. I never thought I'd have to sit across from the boy who was so close to me that I no longer knew where he began and I ended.

"So what are my chances?"

I did not know. Jimmy's academic record was acceptable; his participation in sports reluctant. He had energy, spunk, talent in the arts, and charisma. The committee might just come down harder on him than they would on some kid who had fewer personal resources.

"All I can tell you," I said, "is to write your statement honestly. Write everything, just like you told me tonight. You've got to promise not to try to outslick the committee."

"Are you kidding? I have learned my lesson."

"And don't say that. Everybody says that."

I sat in on Jimmy's D.C. Although he'd never been to the committee before, this was not his first offense. He'd been caught out of the house after hours the year before (headed for my room across the quad). He was known to be flip and sarcastic, to miss commitments. He was black satin in an all-cotton world. I spoke for Jimmy. I tried to show the love and loyalty I knew in him that I suspected the committee might not see for the showmanship.

In a few days Mr. Oates decided that Jimmy would be suspended for a few days, but not expelled. When he returned he was enjoined from leaving the grounds ("Good," he said. "I can't be trusted."), and he was to come up with a plan to make amends to the community. He set to work on a weekend extravaganza of music, dance, and theater. He and I practiced duets together for a chapel program of gospel music, and he even stopped complaining about sports. Jimmy was a changed man, and only occasionally did he liken himself to Winston Smith, the brainwashed main character in *1984*, one of our assigned novels. By spring, his irreverence was back, but so, too, was a new caution. He had come close to leaving St. Paul's, and both of us had been shaken.

Chapter Twelve

I had chosen to apply only to Penn and Princeton, because the recommended five colleges seemed like an admission of doubt or greed; I picked large universities in reaction to St. Paul's intimacy, which was beginning to stifle; Ivy Leagues to satisfy what I thought my advisers expected and to give me career credentials; and mid-Atlantic locations so I'd be close to home if my mother took sick again. I designated Princeton as my first choice, because it seemed to have more prestige, but I had no real preference. I trusted that the fate that had carried me to St. Paul's School would see me on to college.

During spring break, before we received our acceptance letters, fate, in the person of Wally Talbot, rang the phone. I was in the kitchen polishing cabinets. The connection was bad. Wally's voice—familiar at once even though I hadn't heard it since he'd graduated the year before—sounded urgent and far away.

"Listen," he said with little preamble. "I'm working in the admissions department here at Princeton, and I came across your application. From what I can see, it looks like you're in."

"Oh!"

"Don't come. Listen, Libby, whatever you do, don't come.

It's like St. Paul's, only worse. And all the good things about
St. Paul's, it doesn't have. I'm telling you: don't come."

In addition to Wally's oracular call, I saw, when I received
my acceptance letters, that Penn was offering me fifty dollars
more financial aid. I took it as an omen.

Besides, Anthony was going to Penn, too. We fantasized
about the college years ahead. One afternoon he asked jokingly
whether I intended to "pull a St. Paul's" in college. In other
words, did I hope to become a big woman on campus at Penn,
and if so, had I thought about the toll it took on relationships—
including ours?

I felt the constriction in my chest. It forced the air out of
my lungs in little bursts, none of them strong enough to carry
the words I wanted to say: I thought I had been paying attention to our relationship. I thought that he didn't mind what I
did. I thought he liked me for it. As if I'd discovered a brand-
new tactic, I decided that for the moment, I'd let things ride.
September was a long way off.

I concentrated instead on our time together. As the term
wore on, it was true that more students began to act out, and
more Disciplinary Committee meetings filled the evenings. But
we did spend each afternoon together. Out in Pillsbury Field
behind the track, Anthony introduced me to the shot put. After
two years of sports training, I could begin to feel the simple
happiness of exertion. Field gave me the exhilaration of dance,
the wordless joy of translating ideas into movement—but without the complication of an audience. Inside the circle, from
the crouch through the exploding sweep of the pivot, shot put
felt more simple than I'd ever remembered childhood, and as
powerful as I had hoped adulthood might be. For a while, it
seemed as if the buggy, blue afternoons would stretch out in-
definitely, as if in spring term of Sixth-Form year time acquired a half-life that kept graduation always coming, but never
there.

. . .

Then it came. New beds of annuals appeared, the banners were hoisted and the gates swung open to admit the crowds. My family arrived in a caravan of cars: my parents and sister, my grandparents, my aunt Evie and my cousin Dana, friends of the family, and friends of mine, five carloads in all.

My attention swung from my school friends to my family, and then to introducing the two groups. We talked arrangements. Moving so large a group was a complicated operation. The children needed to run and older folks to rest. Those who had not seen the school before wanted to tour. My mother, who was nearly well, wanted to talk. My father craved peace and quiet.

I vacillated between wanting to march them through the rituals—Friday night's dance, chorus and drama performances; Saturday's speeches; the alumni parade; lunch in the Cage next to the gym; crew races; the athletic-award ceremony—and wanting to avoid the rituals myself.

They wanted to get to their motel rooms, unpack, settle in, eat, pour a round of drinks. Several scenarios were offered and rejected. Finally, we did the only sensible thing. We broke into groups and made plans to rendezvous.

Inside North Upper was chaos. Having faced the fact that we were leaving, we seniors were packing like mad, returning items, giving others away, distributing mementoes to our friends like the dying. I stopped every twelve feet for introductions.

"This is my sister, Carole, and my cousins, Dana and Kim."

"Oh, they are so *cute!* Do you like it here? Are you going to come to St. Paul's one day?"

They squirmed under the attention, too well trained to cut and run until they got the signal. They loved the confusion. They picked through the piles of debris in the hallway, and I shushed them when they screeched at a find. We were experienced trash-pickers, conditioned by my mother to cast a gimlet eye over every heap of junk we saw. ("That table? Do you like that table? You know where I got it? . . .") They stood wide-eyed in my room as Alma fussed over them. I could see their eyes scanning the bare walls for a trace of me. They fingered my clothes and blankets and records as if to make real for themselves my presence in this place that had swallowed me up two years before.

Alma's mother arrived, and a general whooping of comingled siblings ensued. Alma's mother sat down—she was tired from the trip—like a woman accustomed to relaxing amid uproar. How different from my mother, who emerged from the car like a Slavonic dance in progress, whirling faster and faster toward evening.

The weekend had that momentum, too. Once the folks had arrived, I was no longer in charge. I was running and running everywhere, trying to stay with them and get to commitments, being driven to the motel and trying to hurry someone to drive me back. I sped like a bicycle down a hill. There was tension between my parents, the same tension I'd always known, but I did not stay still to feel it.

The caravan barely lumbered onto campus for one event before that one finished and another began. By the time we all sat down for the lunch, the caterers were gathering half-eaten trays of cold-cuts. I do not remember whether or not I marched in the parade. I don't think that we went out to the docks for the boat races. My memories of the weekend blur together like a slide show, all colors and no sound, no smells. I do not trust these memories. They are fossils, perfectly laid strata of adolescent fear and anger undisturbed by layers of forgiveness above. My family burst into my School world as if it were theirs. They took over. They set the pace. They were here for a party, and they were having it.

I spent Saturday night at the motel in one of the rooms they had rented. My grandparents went to bed early, but the rest of the entourage stayed up later. They hugged and kissed and celebrated me. I endured the attention I had sought, and I felt like an ingrate.

Church service for the graduating class and family and alumni was to be held the next morning. We talked about attending: who would go, who wanted to sleep late, how early we'd have to arrive to get seats. Finally I told them that I did not want to go. I was tired of St. Paul's School.

"You're on your way," they said.

"You've made connections here that black people have never made before."

"Are you kidding? We never even knew they were there to make!"

"But you're in now, sweetheart. Once you've been kids together, why it's like being in the army. Those are the kinds of contacts you'll call on in later life. You mark my words."

"These people are going back to their own lives after graduation," I said. "I made a few friends, but I do not have any 'contacts,'" I said. My family's fantasies were getting out of hand. What, I wondered, were they expecting of me? How could I ever be grand enough to fit? "What I got is an education."

They listened with expressions of indulgence. Sure, I was tired and grumpy, what with the excitement and all. If I wanted to sleep late on the day of my graduation, well, why not? Hey, they weren't so crazy about dressing up and hustling onto campus, anyway. Whatever I wanted, they said. I'd earned a sleep-in, and they figured I'd attended a mighty lot of Chapel in two years. The party was really going now. Outside in the parking lot came the sounds of merry-making from other Paulie-related lodgers. "Boy, they think they own the joint," somebody said.

"Didn't they rent rooms, too? Don't they have someplace to go?"

Not one thought entered my head that did not seem disloyal. I was ashamed, seeing their pride close up, as if for the first time, at how little I had accomplished, how much I had failed to do at St. Paul's. Somewhere in the last two years I had forgotten my mission. What had I done, I kept thinking, that was worthy of their faith? How had I helped my race? How had I prepared myself for a meaningful future? What plan did I have to make lots of money and be of service? They were right: only a handful of us got this break. I wanted to shout at them that I had squandered it. Now that it's all over, hey, I'm not your girl! I couldn't do it.

I had a spiel about the School's expectations of its students. The School ideal was a perfect being, bright of mind, sound of body, and pure of spirit. None of us made it, I said, that was the con, but we thought we were supposed to. The distance between where we were and the ideal kept us all in a painful reaching, jumping, leaping at the sky. The con was that once in a generation, some freak of nature actually did it, and they put his name on a plaque on the wall so that the rest of us could not claim it was impossible.

I tried the spiel on my family. I tried to lay a bridge of words from my bitterness to their jubilation so that I would not stand so grotesquely alone in their midst. They told me to go to sleep. No wonder I was peevish. It had been a long haul. They'd celebrate for me, as Nana Hamilton once said, until I learned to celebrate myself.

The day of graduation dawned sunny with clouds. We glared at the clouds every half-hour to hold them back. We arrived onto the grounds just before the Chapel service ended. Chapel

Road was lined with expensive cars. My school did not look like itself. I went into the Chapel with my mother. It was packed. We stood in the entryway with other latecomers. I remembered running to Chapel and sitting in the entry, where everyone could see that I was late. I remembered Mr. Tolliver, whom we called Toad, because of his solid body and bad posture, putting his finger into my shoulder. "Girl," he said. "You were late to Chapel."

I was late again, and ashamed, now that I'd stepped through the doors, that I had not had the sense to get there on time. I remembered how the last services of the term had never failed to move me, to help me pass from one phase of my life at St. Paul's to the next. Already, the Rector's voice was intoning the closing prayer. I knew it by heart:

"O God, who through the love and labor of many hast built us here a goodly heritage in the name of thy servant St. Paul, and hast crowned our school with honor and length of days: For these thy gifts, and for thyself, we thank thee, and for past achievements and future hopes; beseeching thee that both we and all who follow after us may learn those things on earth, of which the knowledge continues in thy Heaven. . . .

"Bless the work of this School undertaken for thy glory and continued in thy fear. Make this to be in deed and in truth a Christian school, that none who come here may go away unimproved, that none may be afraid or ashamed to be thy faithful servants."

We sang the *Salve Mater,* which we pulled out only on graduation day, and the traditional closing hymn. The Chapel rang with music. Mr. Wood at the organ, the choir filing out past the throng, singing the song I had sung, dressed in the robes I had worn, the acolytes and the priests, the banners and standards. They filed out smiling, nodding at old students, parents, friends, and singing:

Ye watchers and ye holy ones,
Bright seraphs, cherubim, and thrones,
Raise the glad strain, Alleluia!
Cry out, dominions, princedoms, powers,
Virtues, archangels, angels' choirs,
Alleluia! Alleluia! Alleluia! Alleluia! Alleluia!

It was high-church at its best, and I knew it as well as I knew my mother's voice. I ached with the sound and the sight of it. Distant gobbledegook at first, the seraphs, cherubim, and thrones resonated deeply now. How many times had I argued with that song? Why was it that this rich, rich school had to get dominions, princedoms, and powers to praise their God? Why were our worshippers "disconsolate" while theirs were "gracious" and "bright"? Who had told them that God was pleased with them? Was it the "goodly heritage"? Was that the proof of God's love? Well, what about the rest of the world, whom they asked God not to forget? What about them? What about the dirty, ragged, cramped, stupid, ugly motherfuckers? When would they be crowned with honor and length of days? What made St. Paul's so cocksure? What about the rest of us? What about me?

I cried then because the music was so beautiful and I loved it so, because loving it was treachery, because I had scribbled the words on scraps of paper and looked them up in the dictionary to learn them, because I could not bear to be so far away from a God who smiled on such exquisite praise. I have read the word of the Lord our God until my eyes burned like the very fires of hell. And still you have not found grace? Still not made Tillich's "leap of faith"?

I wanted to leap right then. I wanted to leap into a big, big faith: big as the sky on a black night, big enough to hold Ward A.M.E. and the Chapel of St. Peter and St. Paul within it. I wanted an infinity inside me that could hold it all. I wanted to fly out of my skin, to leave it draped over the chair by the window and fly up into the welcoming night.

I had come to St. Paul's to fly, and I had failed. What had I become that was worthy of so much effort and money?

We went to lunch at the Upper for the traditional poached salmon on red-and-white school plates. At two o'clock I ran to the green behind the Chapel to get in line for graduation.

No music plays as the paired lines move down the hill behind the Chapel and onto the green. The faculty in their caps and gowns proceeded first, and at the end of the faculty file, the Vice-Rectors, the trustees, and the Rector. Then the students. We walked in pairs alphabetically. The clapping rose to a roar as we entered between bleachers arranged in a U facing the dais. We four officers walked at the end of line. My relatives had been waiting, watching for me while more than a hundred students walked past, and they rushed to hoist their cameras to their faces.

The brass ensemble played the *Salve Mater*. We sang it for the second time that day. The Rector and then a guest speaker made speeches. The sun was hot on the top of my head. Prizes and awards lined the long table on the dais. The Rector read the dedication of each before he awarded it to a student. Then, the Vice-Rector stepped to a microphone on the side of the dais opposite the Rector and began calling names of graduating Sixth Formers in flights of four. I was called early, because my last name begins with C. I did not graduate with Honors, not even in English, and I sat stupidly for a moment waiting. There was nothing more. I had simply graduated: no honors.

The Vice-Rector read the diplomas awarded cum laude, magna cum laude, and summa cum laude. I sat still. The sun and my shame made me sweat.

Finally the Rector announced the final awards, those that are given only to graduates. It seemed as if this would never end. I would never get out of the sun and away from the long, long list of students who had done what I had claimed I had come to St. Paul's to do.

"The Rector's Award," said Mr. Oates, "is made at the discretion of the Rector to graduating Sixth Formers whose selfless devotion to School activities has enhanced all our lives and improved the community we share here at St. Paul's School.

"The two students to whom the Rector's Awards are made this afternoon represent a wide variety of characteristics. To be a moment merry, I am going to combine and deliberately mix up comments on their skills and qualities in such a way that I may possibly obscure from you who these students are. Of course, if you care to, you may sort these out as I go, and readily ascertain who they are."

I pursed my lips. "To be a moment merry" indeed. Typical graduation humor. Ha, ha.

"Poised and attractive, determined and responsible, these students have established superior records academically, been an officer of the Sixth Form, become skilled in karate, been outstanding in athletics, sung in the chorus, written for *The Pelican*, been a member of the Missionary Society, joined the Astronomy Club."

My ears perked up at "officer of the Sixth Form." That was one of us four sitting in pairs on either side of the aisle in the front row. I had written articles for *The Pelican*. I shushed the greedy girl within. Starved for some special notice, she stood inside my skin jumping up and down. In the seconds while Mr. Oates read the list, I heard her clamor. I heard how deeply she had been hurt to receive nothing, nothing at all but a diploma. No honors, no cum laude, nothing. Nothing for me, nothing for my work? Not a farthing for my trouble? Nothing for the family who had traveled so far? Nothing to compensate for what they don't even know they have lost—my confidence, my trust? Not one little gift to give the people who have given up a daughter? "I've given her to God," my mother sometimes said. I didn't believe it, because it felt as if she were holding on tighter than ever, but she'd lost me. No matter how dutifully I hid it, it was true.

". . . joined the Astronomy Club."

That was it. None of the other three had ever come out to the observatory. The Astronomy Club was a tiny club. Some of my friends had begun to smile at me. They sought out my eyes. Peter tossed me a happy look. I could not face their eyes. The girl inside was too immodest, too grasping and loud. I looked down into my lap as if folded hands could save me from the discomfiting need within.

"Even-tempered, talented, conscientious, well-mannered, he and he, or he and she, or she and she are students of sterling character and high integrity. St. Paul's is deeply indebted to them."

The Rector called my name. He used all three names, as was the graduation custom. And he called Tom Painchaud's name, too.

I heard clapping, and I got up. Painchaud was coming behind. He and I stood together and received our small white boxes tied in red ribbons. Mr. Oates shook hands with each of us and kissed me. He was beaming as he told us congratulations. I thought of the plane tickets when my mother had been sick. I looked at Painchaud and remembered the friendship he had so freely given on the night of the Sixth-Form elections. After that afternoon I might never see him again. Why had I not talked more with him as we had that night? Why had I been so afraid of his eyes?

I had not loved enough. I'd been busy, busy, so busy, preparing for life, while life floated by me, quiet and swift as a regatta.

I had not loved enough. The greedy girl inside me clutched at the little white box with its red ribbons. She was heartbreaking to look upon, a spoiled child at a party grabbing up expensive gifts, no sooner opened than found wanting, grabbing up new ones, hoping for one that would seep into and fill up her soul.

I had not loved enough.

The old people sang a song in church: "Just As I Am, Without One Plea." We'd sing it as the preacher stood at the altar, in front of the pulpit, calling one, just one, to make the decision to come to God today. "Are you ready?" he asked. "If you had to meet your Maker today, could you say, 'I'm ready, Lord, just as I am? Not as I *hope* to be. Not tomorrow, not tomorrow, brothers and sisters, please. Because tomorrow may never come. 'Just as I am, Thou wilt receive, Wilt pardon, cleanse, relieve.' He wants us as we are. Only one in the world'll take me just as I am! Thank you, Jesus. *Just* as I am. *He'll* make you ready. He can do it. Isn't there one?"

The old people would wave their arms in the air, and I'd never understood. I'd cried and cried at the vision. Just as I was? How I longed to believe it. I'd cried and joined the church. I'd joined the gospel choir—they'd let me, too, at eleven, and I sang with all the adults, hoping that He would fill my soul with belief.

"In every spiritual experience, Tillich says," Reverend Ingersoll had told us, "there must be in the worshipper a 'leap of faith.' "

I had leapt and leapt and leapt, and here I stood, my big feet in white pumps, standing on the ground. How could you leap at the sky?

The Chapel tolled three. The Sixth Form would depart in

half an hour. It said so on the program. The program always said so. It always would. For the first time that year, I was not ready to leave St. Paul's. I had had all my time, all my chances. I could never do it again, never make it right. I had not loved enough.

In the bleachers I saw Nana Jackson, her hands folded in her lap. She was watching the Rector give the last awards. She looked peaceful in her blue and white suit. I remembered how she'd let me play in her hair when I was little, before she cut it, when she took out the hairpins and let it hang down her back. For the last two years, she had sent pear nectar and crackers; cards and money for holidays, even Halloween and Valentine's Day. Pop-Pop had written me faithfully and had ordered stationery for me, white paper with my name and address—ST. PAUL'S SCHOOL—in red.

I was glad of the award in my lap, even though I was no longer satisfied with it. The Rector's Medal—there was only one of those awarded each year, and he was reading it now— carried more prestige. I told myself to be grateful for my award, even though I suspected that it was a booby prize, maybe even the badge of a Tom, a palliative to the selfless-devotion types who fell short of the mark.

Graduation ended abruptly, as always, and we filed past our teachers. We cried and said thank-you. We hugged and walked on to the next teacher. I cried bitterly. I could barely speak to Sr. Fuster, Sr. Ordoñez, Miss Clinton, Mr. Buxton, Mr. Hawley, Miss Deane, Mr. Price, Mr. Shipman, Mr. Oates. Love and gratitude, hate, resentments, shame, admiration, loss. They sloshed on deck in big waves; I could only hold onto the hands that were passing me along the line. Mr. Oates was last. He said things to me, but I could not hear them by now. I could only grasp the last hand, embrace the last body, and let go to step onto the green.

There I grabbed up the children, Carole and Dana and Kim.

They looked with open curiosity at my tears and helped me dry them with their stares. I posed for pictures with India and Alma and Anthony and Jimmy. I stood on the end of bunches of formmates while their parents clicked away. I hugged until my skin tingled. I hugged teary lower formers. Grace was beside herself. Annette let the tears stream down her cheeks.

Parents were rounding us up and herding us into cars. Somebody had to do it. Each hug reminded me of someone I'd missed. Where was Pam Hudson? Had she already gone? Have you seen Painchaud? Did Janie leave yet? Where were Kenny and Ed? Loretta left? And Artie? Where was Michael from the Astronomy Club? Many people did not bother to say goodbye. Someone's parents were giving a big party in New York, and they'd meet up there. Those of us who had come to St. Paul's by accident said good-bye for real. "I'll write you," we promised.

Anthony and I rode with my old high-school friends from Yeadon. Karen and Gary had made the drive themselves in Gary's purple Dodge Duster. The four of us drove to the motel. Now the party took off.

"I graduated, Oh, Lawdy," said a friend of the family whom I called Uncle. "Girl, you tore it up! Me, I was just lucky to graduate, Oh, Lawdy!"

"Get out of here!"

"Honey, that was beautiful. You know, no pomp and circumstance and all that mess. Just simple and elegant."

"Well, hell, they don't need pomp and circumstance. They got the *goods*. As much money and power as they've got, they don't need to advertise."

"That's right. *We're* the ones who need all those caps and gowns and rings and music, because what else you gonna give the young people. God knows half of 'em can't read!"

"Yeah, boy. Dress those children up in all those gowns and crap, and the next week they can't find a job."

"But I surely did love those white dresses. Your girlfriend Alma, was she the one in the long dress?"

"Yep."

"And a flower behind her ear. I like to see that kind of style."

"It's pizzazz."

"It's confidence, and why shouldn't they be confident?"

"And the child with the hat. You know who I mean: blond, kind of plump, pretty face."

"India."

"India, right. You introduced me. She's a doll. I hope you'll keep in touch."

"And Anthony, you looked so tall and handsome coming down the aisle."

"Head and shoulders above the crowd."

Karen and Gary said that they had to begin the drive home. "Some people," Karen said, "are still in school!"

They offered us a ride back to Philadelphia, and we took it. Anthony did not feel as if this were his party, and, of course he was right. The irony was that I did not feel it was mine, either. We left with Karen and Gary after the adults lectured us on being careful and responsible.

"Florence Evans told me this," my mother said. "She told me that once you let that child go, you'll never get her back again."

I gave my mother the little white box of school buttons to keep for me and slunk away from my own party. ". . . Past achievements and future hopes. . . ," I thought. I took with me an envelope that said "Happy Graduation." It was from Mrs. Burrows, the housekeeper at Scudder, and a woman who collected laundry at the gym—a woman whose name I did not even know. Inside was a fresh five-dollar bill. Mrs. Burrows told me that she'd never given a student a graduation present before; no one had ever given her a chance to get to know them.

I kept the envelope in my pocketbook for a long time. I had not passed up all my chances to give love or receive it, and I had the future, at least, to try to do better.

June 1989

Our fifteenth reunion was held at a rustic social club at
the end of a pitted road north of town. One of my
formmates who lived in Concord had arranged for the place.
Inside was a white kitchen, a bar not much bigger than the one
my father built in my grandparents' basement, and a large
main room for eating and dancing. Wrapped around the building was a wide wooden porch that looked onto a pond and
woods.

Tom Painchaud, who also lived in Concord, and worked as
a regional sales supervisor for a beverage distributor, had arranged for the beer. Two kegs sat in the kitchen. The crowd
around them grew big over time.

We arrived just before sunset. The spring had been the rain-
iest in years, and the woods sprouted green and lush. Mosquitoes had been breeding, too. They swarmed us worse than
anyone could remember. As we stood talking in bunches on
the porch and on the green grass, we swatted ourselves. We
looked to see the faces we remembered concealed in the familiar, but different, faces before us, and we swatted each other.
We brushed the mosquitoes tentatively out of each other's hair
and hit them as gently as we could on each other's arms and
necks. We sprayed ourselves from cans of repellent that the
reunion organizers had wisely stationed every couple of feet

along the porch rail. We sprayed each other. And suddenly we were touching again as we had done in earlier times.

"Where are you living?" We asked it of each other just as we had once asked "What house are you in?" It was an opener. You could talk forever about a city or a town. From that start you could get as intimate or remain as distant as you liked.

"Where are you staying this weekend?" The answer to that question could give some indication of an alumnus's present connection to the school. I answered, several times, that my husband and daughter and I were guests of my friends, the Gillespies.

"The Rock? Were you friends with them at school?"

"We became friends when I went back to teach for a year in 'eighty-two. We shared a house. He was the housemaster and I was the second faculty in Corner."

"Whoa! Gillespie ran a tight ship."

"Sure did. You know what I did when I got the letter telling me that I was assigned to Corner, with Cliff as head? I stood in my living room—here I was, a grown woman—and I screamed: 'Oh, no! Not the Rock! How could they have given me the Rock?'

"I was scared to death."

"But it was good?"

"I can't tell you. I learned more about teaching from watching that man in action. Him and Fuster. Opposite ends of the spectrum. But they both pour their souls into teaching."

I had, too. I taught Third-, Fourth-, and Sixth-Formers: essay-writing, Greek mythology, *Huckleberry Finn*, poetry, *Native Son*, *Paradise Lost*, grammar, *Macbeth*, vocabulary, the Book of Job. The chairman of the department was Rich Lederer, the teacher under whom I'd student-taught black literature in my senior year.

The Rector was brand-new. The Reverend Charles Clark was a tall Episcopalian clergyman from California. He'd been the

Dean of the Berkeley Divinity School at Yale, and before that, he and his wife, Priscilla, had worked in the Philippines. Kelly Clark had a West-Coast brand of upper-class elegance that was sunnier and more gentle than the Yankee faculty had come to expect. I watched the upheaval as the old regime gave way. Masters who had long felt stifled sought to establish themselves with the new Rector.

The faculty that had appeared to my teenaged eyes as a monolith of critical white adulthood now revealed itself as a community of idealists, all trying, each according to his or her ability, to help young people. Our job, it sometimes seemed, was to stuff as much Christian charity into our arrogant charges as possible before the world began rewarding them so richly for being so beautiful, charming, and accomplished (which we helped them become).

I felt the zeal of it, the ironic, subversive missionary zeal. I felt the frustration. Like the kids, I stayed up too late. I accepted too many assignments. Like the other faculty members, I exerted too much pressure on my already stress-filled students. Without words, I exuded it like sweat from my pores. No doubt they could smell it on my skin as I bent over their shoulders to point out how they could improve their theses on the third rewrite. And yet, it took all my control to keep from shaking them sometimes, from jacking them up against the wall and screaming into their faces: "Look at what you have here. Buildings, grounds, books, computers, experts, time, youth, strength, ice rinks, forests, radio equipment, observatories. Learn, damn you! Take it in and go out into the world and *do* something."

One afternoon I sat with a student from Japan, listening as she translated into her own language a passage from the *Narrative of the Life of Frederick Douglass,* a book that I had added, with my department chairman's permission, to my Fourth-Formers' readings in American literature. Mochi giggled, at first, to hear Douglass's abolitionist bombast coming from her lips, in her language. I asked her to reread the paragraph. Again and again she repeated the same words. Her voice changed, and her face changed, and I could hear Douglass's passion. The language became transparent for a moment, like the words of an opera. She spoke to me with her voice and her eyes and her body. I felt a jolt of love for this hard-working girl—and, in its wake, a hard knot of feeling toward the black girl who had traveled here from Yeadon ten years before.

Asked to coach an aerobics class ("Oh, by the way, do you think you could help us out with something . . ."), I, who had never taken one, drove into town to buy one of Jane Fonda's books, skimmed it that night, and showed up the next after-noon in the training room at the gym as ill-prepared as my students (most of whom chose aerobics to avoid the standard, competitive offerings). We grunted and groaned through the fall in a regimen that was more akin to boot camp than aero-bics. I watched them resist and yet progress, and I remem-bered when my body, for all its supple youth, had seemed just beyond the reach of reason, a clumsy pet whose care and feed-ing often required more discipline than I could muster; a carnival bumper car that banged from one side of the arena to the other while I spun the steering wheel wildly trying to get control.

I held eighth-period classes in my apartment over tea and coffee, as Sr. Ordoñez had done for us. I watched as Cliff Gillespie sauntered through the hall of our dormitory house, arms out like a cowboy, body upright, ex-Marine straight, roll-ing on the balls of his feet, as capable, in the adoring eyes of the boys, of dispensing praise or blame as a god. They gobbled up his manhood with their eyes and measured themselves against it.

"You're to be in at ten," he said at a house meeting one

night after a few of them ran into the doors, late and laughing, clubby, boyish, defiant. "Ten. You got that? Ten.

"Here. Let me explain it another way. Let me put it so I make myself clear. Ten means ten. Not ten-o-one, not ten-o-two. Ten means ten."

He assigned some punishment jobs, implied that there could be more to come, and strolled back down the hall to his door. I shook my head at them and tiptoed up the stairs to my apartment, which sat atop their rooms. I wanted to leave them alone like new orphans, shocked by the power of Gillespie's censure. Later that term, I used to joke with them, when I was on duty, that "ten means ten." It was a way to let them know that I knew how much they honored their housemaster, and that I was not so big a fool as to envy him their esteem. (They would have punished me for it, and occasionally checked for signs.) I felt love for them as one does for a darling cousin who lives out of town. It surprised me, the first time I felt it, watching them walk to dinner, their ties tied like lumps of coal at their throats.

It surprised me when I felt it for the black kids tumbling noisily over each other's and their own feet, walking close together, joking, teasing, bitching, on their way down the brick path from the Upper, and I could not tell, for a moment, their names, because I was so sure I saw my own schoolmates among them. And then I knew, that the evening sunset at the end of September, the wash of orange on the tall windows of the gray granite library on the pond, was a different sunset, and that I was not in danger of melting into it like a living Dalí painting. I knew that I stood apart from the little crowd wrapping themselves in a cushion of their own voices. I was standing apart, capable of hearing their fear, withstanding their anger, watching the orange sun cling to their smooth cheeks.

The ambitious fifteen-year-old, the West Philly girl transplanted to Yeadon, rushed out of my memory to join them, so that the fat orange sun and the new English teacher's smile could splash on her, too. The adolescent I had been peeked out at me from behind the birches and glared from the shadows of the darkened rooms. She was prideful, funny, ashamed, anxious, cocky, and scared. I had left her alone in New Hampshire, hoping to forget her. Instead she had called me back. She demanded compassion, forgiveness, reunification. When I finished my year of teaching at St. Paul's, I brought the adolescent along.

Two years later, the trustees asked me to serve with them on the Board of Directors. Two trustees from Philadelphia invited me to drive to New Hampshire with them for my first meeting. One was Ralph Starr, who had hosted the recruitment reception where I first met Mike Russell. The other was Kaighn Smith. It had been his wife, Ann, who had asked my next-door neighbor whether she knew any black girls of high-school age who might want to apply to St. Paul's School.

Over the next four years, I traveled to school and to New York for board meetings. During the last two years, I flew to Concord with a board member who chartered a small jet for the purpose. I felt the power of the engine just beyond the gleaming, compact cockpit and its clean-cut pilots. I felt it rise up through the air: smooth air, bumpy air, air with waves and holes and wind like the breath of the God of Israel. I saw New Hampshire miles off, green and russet, red and gold in the fall, green and brown with bursts of pink in spring. And always, the ponds, dark like tea-water, sparkled in the sun and showed the shadows of the clouds. When we dove down toward the earth to land, I felt as fragile as mortality itself.

Once there, we worked in committees. We heard reports. We were taken on tours of the grounds to see work that needed to be done, work in progress, work completed. We met with students and faculty, taking in deference and hostility, answering pointed questions, asking them.

Then, we retired to the long parlor of the Rectory. The walls were papered green as the spring woods and glowed brown with old bookshelves. We listened to more reports. We discussed practical matters and philosophy. We debated about relationships—within the school community, between St. Paul's and other communities; we talked about a new library; we talked about money.

Ralph Starr became my mentor. John Walker, the bishop from Washington, became my guide. I watched John Walker carefully, the way a desert pilgrim stares at an oasis. I wanted to make sure that the blackness, the confidence, the love—not just those qualities, but the coexistence of the three—were real. I wanted to see if it would wither or waver or waffle. It did not.

In the evening, when I met with the black students for a talk and dessert, I would take John Walker's confidence with me. I held onto it, and it steadied me as I met the hungry eyes of the young people who draped themselves defiantly over red leather chairs. I could see fear in their eyes as surely as John must have seen it in mine. Who was this person who walked about in the white world? And at what price? What did it mean to be black in America if it did not mean handicap, shame, or denial?

"Did you like it here?"

"How'd you get on the board?"

"Why did you come back to teach?"

"If you had it to do over, would you come here again?"

"Would you send *your* daughter to St. Paul's School?"

For a while at the reunion, I simply stopped talking. I ate dinner. I smiled. I braved the mosquitoes to walk around the porch. It seemed as if I'd been explaining half my life. Weren't we trying to understand each other fifteen years before? Hadn't we been standing on the same cliffs, screaming at each other across the same divide? Suddenly it felt pointless to keep talking, naive. Under the canopy, mosquitoes, thick as smoke, made a black cloud over the steaks like some moral to an African folktale I dimly knew.

I could not begin to explain how I had felt that afternoon on Cliff and Alina Gillespie's screen porch as I sat next to Rafa Fuster, who was retiring. I could not explain the sincerity of Cliff Gillespie's interest in the news about my schoolmates: José Maldonado, a special narcotics prosecutor for the City of New York; Ed Shockley, a playwright; Grace Tung, a hospital administrator; Annette Frazier, an investigator of human-rights violations for the State of Illinois; Kenny Williams, a gas-company manager in Philadelphia; Michael Russell, an advertising executive; Janie Saunders, a New York banker; Peter Starr, a professor of comparative literature in California; India Bridgeman, a Los Angeles dance critic; Alma Howard, an attorney with a health-maintenance organization in Watts; Jimmy Hill, a New York restaurant manager; Anthony Wade, a program officer in a private foundation. Lee Bouton, who graduated ahead of me, dropped out of her university to work, then enrolled in college in her thirties and was thriving. Bernard Cash, who returned to St. Paul's to teach after ten successful years in White Plains, New York, classrooms, left SPS suddenly, for "personal reasons," as the administration explained after he was gone, in the winter term of his first year.

At the reunion the interest in each other's news took on a more competitive edge, a shorter perspective.

In the course of the evening, we met each other's spouses, those who had come. Some had connections to St. Paul's or other prep schools. Some did not, but were curious. Anthony's wife told him that she'd rather not stand around all evening playing "thirtysomething," a reference to a current yuppie-style television series. My husband joked that he wanted me to be free to "work the crowd." He took our daughter to a new, deluxe, yellow-plastic playground outside a local fast-food restaurant and went back to the Gillespies' to put her to bed.

Wayne Gilreath and his wife had brought their baby, a bright-eyed little man whom I danced with, holding him high in my arms. Wayne had been an even-tempered president of the Third World Coalition during our Sixth-Form year, and was now a TV news director in Baltimore. The baby looked very much like his outgoing wife. I stuck my name tag on the baby's chest and took it back. He retrieved it from me and wore it. An hour later I came back in from the porch to find his tiny chest plastered with names. He was all of us at once.

One woman talked earnestly about how her decision to buy an automobile had become a political act, a watershed in her friendship with an ethnic woman. " 'When you have children,' I told her, 'you look around for the most crash-worthy car.' " To the friend, however, a Volvo station wagon meant more. We probed delicately around a discussion of how what we own tells who we are.

Another woman told me she'd just returned from visiting a friend whose daughter had died suddenly. We talked about grief and love.

Anthony described his work in philanthropy. He was on a one-man mission to reform public education, and he was doing it with private money. "So what about you?"

I said I was writing a book about our time at St. Paul's.

"Are you exposing any secrets?"

"You better hope the hell not," someone leaned over and shouted at Anthony.

Several classmates asked why I'd returned to teach. I responded several ways, all more or less true: that I'd needed a breather between marriages—and the spiritual healing of service; that I'd wanted to revisit the place that had so disturbed me in my overserious youth; to encourage kids who might feel similarly; and to learn from them.

"Wasn't it weird going back?"

"What's weird is how the times shuffle in my mind," I said. It was hard to keep talking over the noise. I made a soft, chopping motion with my hand to try to convey the folding of cards in a deck. I was thinking about a quieter discussion I'd had that afternoon with Bruce Chan on the Gillespies' screen porch.

Bruce talked about his work for the district attorney's office. "My girlfriend's an ophthalmologist," he said. "It's great. People come to see her, and they go away happy. I see my clients right in the middle of the worst possible times of their lives. No matter what happens, they're enraged when they come to see me, and just about the best I can hope for is that they are merely angry by the time it's over. Helluva way to make a living."

He thought it was good that one of us ethnic alumni had made the commitment to work with St. Paul's, but the fact of the matter was that he did not know if it was worth it. "I mean, there's so much here, it seems almost like a waste to come back here and give more. It's good for the minority kids, I'm sure. I would have loved to know that there was an alumna, somebody who knew the score, speaking for me on the board, or coming to visit. But there's so much to do outside this . . . bubble. I wonder if we aren't practically obliged to give it back elsewhere, to people who never got it in the first place."

"I do give it back elsewhere," I said. I was glad that I felt no anger. I had heard the argument in my mind so many times. Now there was no anger, and I could smile. "But I don't feel that there's anything wrong in giving it here, too. It is like admitting who I am. I came here, and I went away changed. I've been fighting that for a long time, to no purpose. I am a crossover artist, you know, like those jazz musicians who do pop albums, too."

My mind had drifted for a moment as I thought of my white husband, a man raised in a small town in Iowa.

"I used to hate those musicians for that. I wouldn't buy any more of their records because they were no longer pure. Well, I didn't leave here pure. This is who I am."

I wondered whether "crossover" was the word I wanted. Did it convey enough tension? Or did it sound like dying a cultural death into a choir of black preppies standing on a riverbank, beige corduroy wings to match their trousers, singing: *My heart looks back and wonders how I got oooo-over. . . .* Wrong image. I wanted an image of wholeness, inclusion: moving circles that come together, overlap, drift apart. Why else were we, like married women, so concerned to find the right compounds and hyphenates? Black American (big B, small b), Afro-American, Afric-American, people of color, Afro-Caribbean, Anglo-African, people of the diaspora, African-American.

I went at it another way.

"I make the choices every day—to live where my kid grows up with black people like the black people I grew up with, and to hope that she doesn't get burned up by the shame."

(Could Bruce know what I meant by shame? The shame that made us unable to look upon our own children: "You seen her baby?"

"Uh-huh. Thought I was at the zoo."

"When I looked in that stroller, baby all dolled up in lace and all, all I could say is: 'Sure is clean.' "

Could Bruce know that while black intellectuals debate the impact of the 1960s on black self-image, people on my street still say a baby looks like a monkey if she's too dark? Could he hear little girls cry out to God in the dark for good hair? Were there Chinese-American equivalents?)

That's what I thought about when I looked at my form-mates across the table. It had been hard enough to try to communicate with Bruce, who cared, passionately, about the morals of ethnicity. I couldn't summon the words to explain again just to make conversation. My mind continued idly shuffling still photos of the past. I chopped at the air with my hand.

Anthony motioned me to come outside. We sprayed each other with repellent. We sprayed the air. Anthony asked what I was drinking. "Bottled water," I said. "That's the extent of it."

He raised his eyebrows.

"I don't drink," I said.

"Not at all?"

I laughed. "Under any and all circumstances I don't drink." It felt good to talk simply after a day of complicated explaining. We had done what people do at fifteenth reunions: spread out selected highlights of our lives for our classmates to admire or share. Now the night came down around us. The party changed. We began to tell each other about our divorces, our disillusionments, our fears.

"It means what it sounds like. I don't drink anymore. It's OK, really, once you know."

He went inside and came back with two bottles of water.

"So what else did you find out writing this book?"

"Life is like a leaf!"

He coughed out that big laugh of his. "Don't start! I can't take it."

"No, listen. Seriously. It's a whole book of life is like a leaf. That's what got me through St. Paul's. It was stored up like a present from a willful, ambition-driven girl to the woman she would become. Do you remember how much I hated Mr. Shipman?''

"Do I?''

"When I went back to teach—you know how it is. There's the opening-night party in the Gates Room. Mr. Shipman came over to me and welcomed me back, just as nice. And I thought: 'Doesn't this man know how much I hated him? Doesn't he remember that he *failed* me? Coming up to me like an old friend.'

"Then he said he was going to give me one piece of advice— that you know you've been at St. Paul's too long when the stuff that sixteen-year-olds say starts to make sense. And he laughed. I'd never seen the man laugh.''

Anthony put his head back. He liked a story, always had. "What you're talking about is grace," he said.

"Is it?''

I like the simplicity of the word. Old ladies in church use it. Old drunks who don't drink anymore use it. Grace, Tillich says, is accepting that you are accepted. Children say grace at table. Bosomy blond Baptists and tweedy Episcopalians use it. Teenagers are the only ones who shun the word, as if it might snatch from them the magic of their power.

Later that night, another friend asked me what the hardest thing was about writing about St. Paul's. "The hardest part is writing about my family," I said.

"Really? Not St. Paul's?''

"St. Paul's is the setting. It's the place, not the main character.''

The music was going by then, loud, loud, loud like the old days, the same undanceable rock. People danced to it, torsos bolt upright, knees kicking, legs jumping, hippity-hoppity like an Appalachian buck dance.

It was cool outside. Woozy mosquitoes floated through a haze of insect repellent and cigar smoke. The porch emitted a corona of light into the darkness, beyond which the ponds spread out smooth and black.

I recalled my great-grandfather's stories that I had used for comfort that night when I'd sat out on the ice. "Jump, Izzy, jump. Papa'll catch you. . . ." The white dog in the cane field; the witch outside the door; "Skin, skin, ya na know me?" Those were as easy to write as to tell, but not the rest of it, not the betrayal. The hard part is to find the words to say it outright: that Pap was wrong. His stories taught me fear and shame and secrecy. "Trust no man." But I cannot throw them out. I cannot escape into some other history of my own choosing, one where the African princess is carried out of slavery at a young age by the gentle Seminoles, where she learns to hunt and fish and bear beautiful brown babies under the Spanish moss. Get serious. I've been given my stories, and in them, people who try to fly are burned out of their own skins.

What my stories do is tell me why—why the old people looked at us with such unforgiving eyes, why they pushed us away, but wouldn't let go. Without the stories, I'd have nothing to explain the cacophony in my head in the indigo New Hampshire night. I'd be back to fifteen years old, sitting in the Art Building's common room, feeling the crazy panic again, hearing the white kids telling me to buck up because slavery's past, Jim Crow's dead and gone without a trace. Jump, Izzy.

Nowhere else will I get the rhythm of these stories, the ghosts and their magic. That's hard to write, too. It's hard to write about a community of souls, living and dead, white dogs that scream like women, barracudas that follow swimmers like angels to keep them safe. It's hard to tell it in mixed company without beginning the old explanations again, the old defensiveness and inarticulate rage. Take away the ooga-booga stuff, and Toni Morrison would be fine, a girl once whispered to me in college. Without the stories and the songs, I am mute. A white American education will never give them to me; but it can—if I am graced, if I do not go blind in the white light of self-consciousness, if I have guides before me and the sense to heed them—it can help me to see the stories, growing like a vine out of the cane fields, up out of unmarked graves, around my soul. It can help me search out the very history it did not teach me. "Let us learn those things here on earth," proclaims the school motto, "the knowledge of which will continue into the heavens."

St. Paul's gave me new words into which I must translate the old. But St. Paul's would keep me inside my black skin, that fine, fine membrane that was meant to hold in my blood, not bind up my soul. The stories show me the way out. I must tell my daughter that. I must do it so she'll know. Then I can go to my own room where the window is open to the black night and fly out unafraid to meet the darkness. I can fly out at dark to rub against the open sky. And ain't I a voman? I must leave my mother and father. I must leave my husband and daughter sleeping. They will come, too, if they want. The night can carry us all. It is big enough. Others are there already, calling, welcoming. At dawn I will alight on my sill. I can slip into my smooth black skin. It will welcome me. I will stay within it most nights, and sleep next to my husband, but I will return again and again to the sky. The skin will grow wrinkled as the nights come and go, but my husband will not salt it. My skin will know me, and I will not have to fear my skin.

I did not ask for the stories, but I was given them to tell, to retell and change and pass along. (Each one teach one, pass it on, pass it on.) I was given them to plait into my story, to use, to give me the strength to take off my skin and stand naked and unafraid in the night, to touch other souls in the night. This time Izzy will jump of her own will when her legs have grown strong enough to absorb the shock; she will not lie on the ground, splayed out alone, crippled by distrust. She will learn how to jump through life, big, giant jumps. She'll fall, and get up again. Up, Izzy, up. Paint, dance, read, sing, skate, write, climb, fly. Remember it all, and come tell us about it.

I have never skated on black ice, but perhaps my children will. They'll know it, at least, when it appears: that the earth can stretch smooth and unbroken like grace, and they'll know as they know my voice that they were meant to have their share.

ABOUT THE AUTHOR

Lorene Cary was graduated from St. Paul's School in 1974 and received a B.A. and M.A. from the University of Pennsylvania in 1978. After graduate study at the University of Sussex, in England, she worked as a writer for *Time* and as an Associate Editor at *TV Guide*. Her short fiction has been published in *Obsidian*. Ms. Cary lives in Philadelphia with her husband, R. C. Smith, and their daughter, Laura.